women's SOCCER

THE GAME AND THE 1999 FIFA WOMEN'S WORLD CUP

ONE DAY A WOMAN will appear who is fast and strong and can make a ball spin into whichever part of the back of the net she chooses. She will be so talented that to exclude her will break equal opportunities law, and the European Court of Human Rights will insist that she be given a chance to prove herself at the highest level. There will only ever be one woman like this but the fear that there will be more will tear at men's hearts and egos. She will be the biggest star in the game's history, she will be rich, she will be loved to her face and hated behind it. International goalkeepers will shoot themselves for failing to save her sweetly struck shot from 35 yards out that wins her team the Champions League and then the Super Cup. Her colleague's girlfriends will storm out of the stadium when the men embrace her at the final whistle. Football-mad geneticists will wonder which player should fertilize her eggs to create the greatest footballer that ever lived. She will retire at the peak of her game and successfully manage a lower league side, taking it far enough to rub shoulders with and rile Manchester United, while just occasionally coming on as a sub to score the winner if necessary. That woman will not be me. But I doubt her joy will be any more intense than the happiness I feel when I am just about acceptable on the soccer field.

—Alyson Rudd, *Astroturf Blonde*

women's
SOCCER

THE GAME AND THE 1999 FIFA WOMEN'S WORLD CUP

FOREWORD BY MARLA MESSING AND DONNA DE VARONA
INTRODUCTION BY HANK STEINBRECHER
EDITED BY JIM TRECKER AND CHARLES MIERS
PRINCIPAL PHOTOGRAPHY BY J. BRETT WHITESELL

UNIVERSE

We would like to thank Elizabeth Van Itallie for her patience, goodwill, and talents; the fine authors and players, from all over the world, who put time aside to contribute to the book; Jim Moorhouse, Brian Remedi and Cathy Christensen at U.S. Soccer; Aaron Heifetz, Steve Vanderpool, Marla Messing, Donna DeVarona and Brett Lashbrook at the 1999 FIFA Women's World Cup Committee; Ralph Irizarry and Leah Steele at ROI Marketing.

First published in the United States of America in 1999
by UNIVERSE PUBLISHING
A Division of Rizzoli International Publications, Inc.
300 Park Avenue South
New York, NY 10010

00 01 02/ 10 9 8 7 6 5 4 3 2

Printed in England

Library of Congress Catalog Card Number: 98-61893

Design: Elizabeth Van Itallie / Hello Studio

Text credits: First page and last page quotes by Alyson Rudd, excerpted from *Astroturf Blonde, Up Front and Onside in a Man's Game*, Headline Book Publishing 1998, reprinted by permission of Alyson Rudd. "Ann Lisseman: Police Officer, Defender," excerpted from *I Lost My Heart to the Belles* by Pete Davies, William Heinmann Ltd in 1996 and Mandarin Paperbacks in 1997, reprinted by permission of Pete Davies. "Familiar Anonymous Ecstasy," excerpted from *Perfect Pitch 3: Men and Women,* edited by Simon Kuper and Marcela Mora y Araujo, Headline Book Publishing 1998, reprinted by permission of Headline Book Publishing.

Principal photography provided by: J. B. Whitesell / International Sports Images.
Credits accompany photographs except those listed below. The publisher has made every effort to identify copyright holders of materials in this book. Any omission or exclusion is regretted and can be included in future printings.

Front cover: The U.S. Women's National Team in the 1996 Olympic Games. (Allsport) Back cover: The U.S. Women's National Team Training Equipment. (Andy Lyons, Allsport) Page 1: Youth player. (Bild Byran) Pages 2-3: Training the goalkeeper. (Doug Pensinger, Allsport) Pages 6-7: Young player on the field. (Richiardi) Page 10: Nigeria's goalkeeper congratulates her teammate. (Bild Byran) Page 85: Gro Espeseth. (Courtesy Gro Espeseth)

FOREWORD

DREAM TEAMS HAVE COME and gone over the years. Thrown together for a brief time, they flash brightly in an Olympics or a world championship, only to go their separate ways afterwards, not having made a tangible difference in the growth of their respective sports.

But since 1985, when the U.S Women's National team was first formed and a soccer supernova named Michelle Akers was added to the squad, no group of individuals has made a longer, or a more lasting impact, on the landscape of women's sports in the United States.

By 1991, when the U.S. won the first Women's World Cup in China, current stars such as Mia Hamm, Julie Foudy, Brandi Chastain, Joy Fawcett, Kristine Lilly, and Carla Overbeck were not only on the roster but seasoned veterans. They inspired young girls who would later become teammates and together in front of 76,418 fans in Atlanta, they won an Olympic gold medal in 1996 and inspired a nation.

The team's rise in popularity over their 14-year existence parallels the climb in youth soccer league participation among young girls. While other sports feel the need to "reconnect" with their fans, this team, for all intents and purposes, is on a first-name basis with its supporters, giving freely of their time, signing the extra autographs.

When the FIFA Women's World Cup came to the United States last summer, a large amount of the credit for how big this event became belongs to this extraordinary team. It would be unthinkable, even just a few years ago, to imagine a women's sporting event that would be played in major U.S. stadiums with all 32 of its matches nationally televised.

Sepp Blatter, the new president of FIFA, has often been quoted as saying "the future of football is feminine." For those of us fortunate to be associated with the U.S. Women's National Team, the future has been now for a long time. ∎

Marla Messing
President and Chief Executive Officer
1999 FIFA Women's World Cup Organizing Committee

Donna DeVarona
Chairman
1999 FIFA Women's World Cup Organizing Committee

SOCCER

WOMEN

INTRODUCTION
OUR WOMEN'S DESTINY
BY HANK STEINBRECHER

THE DAWNING OF A new age is upon us in 2000. The signs have been there for a number of years now. The progress made has been remarkable. The road traveled, nothing short of glorious.

And now, as the millennium dawns, the U.S. Soccer family is embarking on a journey like no other.

Without question, the 1999 Women's World Cup was the most successful women's sporting event ever held. It won't matter how you measure it, the foundation for success has already been laid. From sponsorships, to tickets sales, to media exposure: the foundation is firm.

When scores of thousands of fans filed into Giants Stadium in the New Jersey Meadowlands on June 19 to cheer on the U.S. Women's National Team in the first match of the tournament, history had already been made.

The buzz surrounding the tournament had captivated thousands of fans and journalists from around the U.S. Even the doubters in the media sat up and took notice when the pageantry and success from the first match became apparent.

Women's soccer was destined to be the catalyst for women's sports in America when the USA shocked the world by winning the inaugural Women's World Cup in 1991. Since that time, the team has known success at every level.

And it hasn't been done in front of just a small "niche" audience, although clearly the team has gained cult status among many young players. The Women's National Team has gained in stature every year of their existence, with attendance and media exposure continuing to increase.

In 1998, the U.S. women played in front of an average crowd of 15,467 fans, the highest total in their history. Across the last five years, the U.S. has, incredibly, played in front of an average crowd of 11,477. An amazing total for any women's sporting event in this day and age.

Across the 1990s the U.S. Women's National Team has become the definition of success in the world of women's soccer. Now, it is synonymous with the success of women's sports worldwide. ■

Hank Steinbrecher is the General Secretary of the United States Soccer Federation.

From Morocco to the United States, women's soccer is becoming an integral part of every country's culture. (*Opposite*: Popperfoto; *above*: Michelle Akers, International Sports Images)

EDITOR'S NOTE

BY JIM TRECKER

THE 1999 FIFA WOMEN'S WORLD CUP was in itself a significant event to be sure. But, seen in a broader context it was another chapter in the women's sports story whose modern roots extend to the historic Title IX legislation in the 1970s and now is inspiring the women of all the world.

The United States has always been a leader in women's sports, but until Title IX required that female athletes be afforded appropriate programs and financial support alongside that traditionally given to men, the games were frequently played in informal and "club" style competitions. Within just two decades women's sports leagues now abound, command national television contracts, and female athletes are providing role models for millions of young athletes worldwide.

Nowhere has the growth and acceptance of women athletes been better demonstrated than in soccer. The college game flourishes nationwide and the W-League, the post-collegiate women's league, has enjoyed modest, steady growth in its early stage. U.S. Soccer, the country's governing body for the sport, is engaged in a thorough study of how to launch a professional league along the lines of Major League Soccer. The Women's World Cup propelled women's soccer into the international spotlight, and it seems that a pro league is inevitable.

This book is about soccer but it is really a celebration of all the women who have opened an entirely new team sports spectrum in recent years. Individual women have been internationally prominent throughout much of the century—Sonja Henie, Babe Didriksen, Mary Lou Retton, among them—but only now are the team sports reaching these heights. American basketball, soccer, and softball teams were gold medal winners at the 1996 Olympics. We can see this is only the beginning.

The women's soccer realm is dotted with special people who have important ideas and resolve. Julie Foudy is front and center in the fight against heinous child labor practices; Egypt's Sara Mohammed has bravely put women's soccer on the map in her nation, where Arabic tradition creates special challenges for women playing sports; Michelle Akers sits on the prestigious FIFA Football Committee, where she will have a voice in how the international governing body leads the game into the next millennium. You will meet many other people we can truly consider heroes among the women in this book.

As in so many pursuits, America currently occupies the world leadership position in women's soccer. Young women from around the world have entered our universities to pursue the game they love—in fact Laurie Hill of Mexico polished her game at the University of California at Santa Barbara in the early '90s, and Lene Terp, captain of Denmark, also followed the United States college path. Kelly Smith's story, in this book, is truly representative of these opportunities.

A nationwide commitment exists for women's sports. It is clearly a meaningful part of American society and is a symbol of how much the United States is among the world leaders in all feminine issues. The 1999 FIFA Women's World Cup and its attendant events were in part a watershed and in part an underscoring of this philosophy. ■

the women's
GAME

THE HISTORY
OF THE WOMEN'S GAME AND THE WORLD CUP

BY ELIO TRIFARI

ANYONE AIMING TO TRACE the real history of women's soccer should first study how the feminist movement has emerged as an integral component of society. Today it's normal to look at girls playing basketball or softball, running, or kicking soccer balls in leagues and schools in the United States or even in the rural communities of Africa. Yet this all happened only with sacrifice and a constant struggle to make sport truly universal—more or less what happened in politics, economics, and social life during the course of the last century. It was only in 1972 that the United States approved Title IX as general law, introducing gender equity into college sports and other campus activities.

Today's remaining negative attitudes about women in sports are vestiges of the attitudes that have historically excluded women from participating in sports. The Greek poet Homer writes of girls only being allowed to gently pass a ball to one another in royal palaces. Grace and elegance were the unique requisites of such a "game" at the end of second millennium B.C., while men were asked to display strength and ability in a variety of gestures organized in a competitive manner.

Looking at early reports of structured sports activities, we can say that women may have participated in "mob" games, the well-named rough and tumble versions of football/soccer played between opposing villagers as early as the twelfth century, and probably even before, but we have very few reliable or accurate records of such matches. However, we can agree with Scottish historians when they describe competitions between single and married women at the end of the last century as the first appearance of a "modern" ball game not exclusively reserved for men. The game, in which an inflated pig bladder was used as the ball, was first played at an annual celebration in Inverness, near the famous Loch Ness. This women's competition became a regular event in Scotland at the same time that men's football—as English-speaking countries of Europe called the game—was rapidly spreading around the globe.

In the early twentieth century, the women's game achieved a certain measure of popularity in England, France, and Canada. There was a sort of golden age for women's soccer, and during World War I, when no British men's games were held, there were significant charity exhibition competitions held to raise funds for the Red Cross, with at least one game attended by about 50,000 people. Some Eastern European countries also hosted ladies' games, often defying civil

The women's game evolved from a sporadic amateur game to a professional and international sport. *Opposite:* A goalkeeper in action for Eves of the Apple Packers in 1953. (Popperfoto) *Top:* An 1895 illustration of the British Ladies Football Club. (Popperfoto) *Above:* Lecas Inland Revenue plays against Leeds G.P.O. in a 1961 match. (Popperfoto) *Center:* Captain April Heinrichs celebrates the team victory of the North American Cup. (Phil Stevens Photography) *Below:* Germany's Meinert exults in the semi-finals of the 1995 World Cup. (Richiardi)

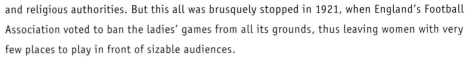

Women around the world make history. *Above:* Norway celebrates winning the 1995 FIFA Women's World Cup. (Chris Cole, Allsport) *Left:* Japan's goalie Junko Ozawa communicates with her team in a 1996 Olympic Games match. (Allsport) *Middle:* China's goalie, Hong Gao, consoles her teammates after defeat in the finals of the 1996 Olympic Games. (Bild Byran) *Bottom:* Denmark and Norway. (Al Bello, Allsport)

and religious authorities. But this all was brusquely stopped in 1921, when England's Football Association voted to ban the ladies' games from all its grounds, thus leaving women with very few places to play in front of sizable audiences.

During the same period, intramural soccer games frequently took place in U.S. high schools and colleges: yearbooks and school records dating to 1930, or even before, describe prizes and results of women's soccer games held during the parents' or exhibition days of this or that institution. But given the power of England in the international governing bodies of the sport at that time, the Football Association ban was a terrible knockout blow for the women's movement, and—with the exception of a few countries like France, where the first sanctioned women's match was held in Paris in 1929, or Italy, where a national league was formed in 1933—we have to wait until after World War II to experience a revival of women's soccer. This time momentum was generated not only in English-speaking countries, but also in Northern Europe, notably in Scandinavia and Germany. In Italy, where there was already a tradition of women playing the game, a national association was founded in 1950 by Countess Angela Altini di Torralbo, but in fact even this was restricted to playing in certain regions of the country. Germany made a step forward, organizing the first unofficial European championship in 1957 in West Berlin; 11 years later, another Italian women's federation was founded and a league was formed. The first Italian title was won by a team from Genoa—most appropriate, as it was Genoa F.C. which had won the first men's Italian title 70 years before. Two other federations were subsequently formed, and the three groups merged in 1972 to form one of Europe's most organized leagues.

England's Football Association lifted its ban in 1970, and it quickly became clear that women's football could become a legitimate contender for women's sports passions: by the beginning of the 1970s, there were organized soccer leagues for women in 35 countries. Germany organized another unofficial European championship in 1970; Mexico hosted an unofficial world championship in 1971, one year after hosting the men's World Cup. Opportunities were being created and the word was spreading. Things, however, were far from easy. Women's soccer was little more than a curiosity, the level of play was unsophisticated, and looking at ladies' matches was often described as like seeing a men's competition in slow motion. Moreover, there was little or no knowledge of how to develop skills for such a game, no dedicated coaches, few places to play, and a debilitating sense of organizational improvisation.

Nevertheless, some determined and brave women persisted. The 1980s saw a proliferation of official matches between national teams in Europe: 1984 was the year of the first officially sanctioned European Championship for national teams. Two years later, during the general assembly of FIFA—the world soccer governing body—in Mexico, Norway's representative Ellen Wilde strongly encouraged delegates to recognize women's soccer: the answer was the first World Tournament, an "experiment" held in 1988 in the Guangdong province of mainland China. The same country was awarded the honor of hosting the first World Cup three years later.

Not only was this tournament exciting, well attended, and successful for the organizers, there was a significant added bonus: the women's team from the United States won. The win in that competition was the turning point for women's soccer. Now it was logical to ask the Inter-

CREATING A TEAM
BY SHEILA EDMUNDS

Sheila Edmunds is the founder of the most successful women's club team in Britain, the Doncaster Belles, whose members now field girls and women's teams from age ten to thirty-eight. Although women's clubs are now starting to receive modest attention and support in England, the country that invented the game had rarely paid attention to the women's game. It was only in 1993 that the Football Association (the organization whose name itself gave us the very word soccer*) assumed responsibility for developing the women's game. In a land with 92 men's professional league clubs and hundreds more Football Association clubs, from 1921 until 1970 women were not allowed to play in any of these stadiums. A true pioneer in the sport, Sheila and her husband, Paul, coached the Belles' team to two Premier League titles and six Women's F.A. Cup Finals. But first, they had to find a place to play. . . .*

When we started the football club, in 1969, I don't think any of us ever thought that women's football would reach its present-day status as an organized spectator sport. We were all keen and eager to play this wonderful game, but we weren't at all ready for the problems it would bring.

Initially we had to overcome both the prejudice against women playing football and the casual but continuous sexist remarks made, it sometimes seemed, by every official and every passerby we saw. Barriers had to be broken, and some took a long time to break. As pioneering players we had to work and pay for everything ourselves. Club funds were nonexistent. The players had to do a lot of fundraising, and sponsorship had never been heard of or thought of before. In fact, we had to start by thinking up everything from scratch, from purchasing equipment and uniforms to organizing matches. The club owned very few footballs for training, so we all took our own, and the club bought the match balls. Once we had designed the club's badge and agreed on the color scheme, uniforms were also bought at our own expense.

Finding somewhere to play was the greatest of our problems. The powers that be did not want women playing on their pitches, so we had no choice other than to play in the local parks. Eventually we were allowed to reserve a town pitch, but as soon as we'd paid for it we realized that there were no separate changing facilities for women, and men, who used adjacent pitches at the same time, were also using the changing rooms. So playing times were affected by when the men were using the facilities.

In the winter, training was an even greater problem. Sport arenas and gymnasiums were difficult to rent. There always seemed to be no availability, and the prices were high.

This left us outside, in the dark, at the local park. We used the small amount of light the streetlights nearby emanated to do fitness work, but we had to forget about practicing ball skills.

Initially our coaches, trainers, and managers were all friends, boyfriends, and husbands. Once standards improved, our skills and fitness needed to improve in line with the opposition so we advertised in our local newspaper for a professional coach and eventually, in 1974, we got one.

After playing charity games and friendly matches for a year or two, we joined a league, the Sheffield Ladies League. Six teams were in this league, coming from towns up to 50 miles apart. Participating in a league meant we played away from home and for that we needed transportation, which meant more money. We shared all our cars and all the ones our friends and family could spare and then split the cost of petrol between us. We finally progressed to using a minibus for away games. This was advantageous because often (especially when our opponents gave us poor directions) we had to use the bus as our locker room and change en route. Without family support I don't think the club would have survived.

In 1983 after much pain, heartache, and determination, we won our first major cup final—the Women's Football Association Trophy (a national competition). As winners we were invited to represent England in a European club championship tournament held in Holland (with each player responsible for paying her own way). We really thought now we had made it. However, when we arrived in Holland we realized how far behind other European countries we were in terms of funding, sponsorship, training, and support. We were the poor relations. We won the Fair Play Award, but we finished in sixth place out of six in the tournament.

But none of the problems we experienced took away our passion and determination to go on. Our love of the game brought us all closer together as a team and gave us a lot of hope, spirit, and enjoyment. There were a lot of hardships we needed to survive, but I am very glad I was there at the time. ■

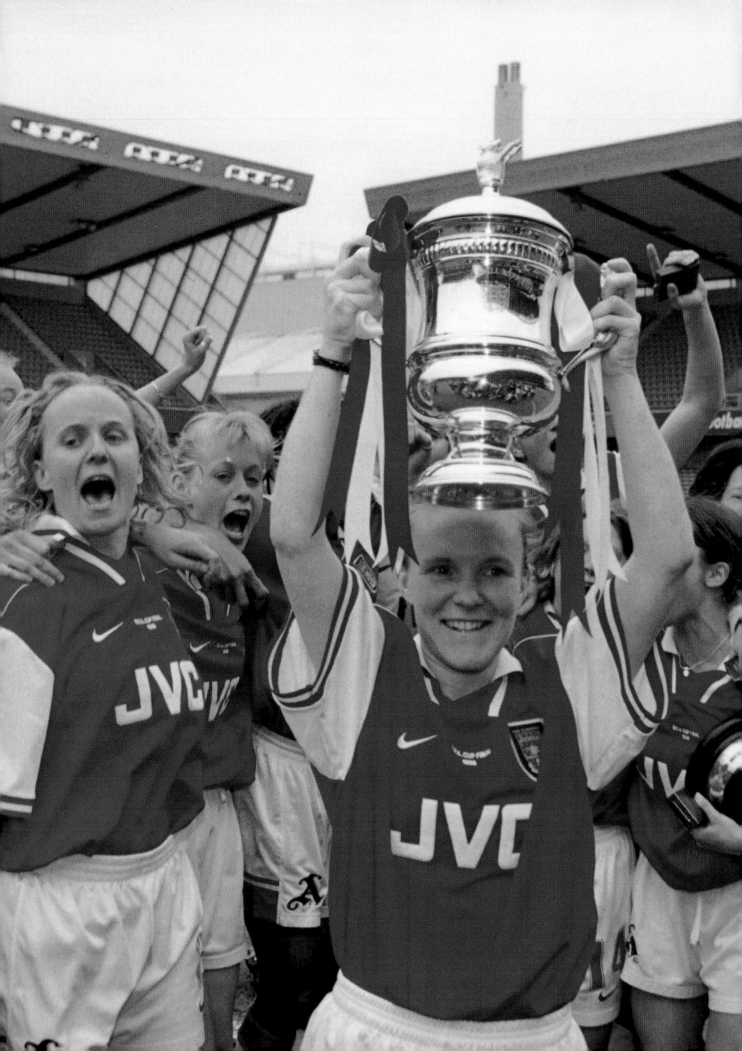

national Olympic Committee to add women's soccer as an official sport to the 1996 Olympic Games, to be held in Atlanta, Georgia. The live spectacle that ensued as the U.S. team defeated China to win the Olympic gold medal set the stage perfectly for the third edition of the FIFA Women's World Cup, which has arrived just after a U.S. Women's National Team vs. World All-Star game in San Francisco: all signs that women's soccer can be considered a leading sports discipline throughout the world.

Thanks to American girls (about 7 million play soccer) the total number of registered players has reached about 32 million worldwide, in more than 102 countries (the men's game is organized in 198 FIFA recognized countries). As a result, women are starting to have their own referees, coaches, trainers, and dedicated fans. Women's soccer is helping FIFA spread the game further: Oceanic and Asian countries are introducing women's soccer into their culture, and Africa is starting to explore its huge, almost completely hidden potential.

Soccer is also evolving on the technical side: not only as an also-ran to the men's game but as a game with its own integrity and style. If its rhythms and intensity differ from the way the top professional men play the game, supreme technical ability and fair play are emerging as leading characteristics. There are still a lot of soccer-oriented countries, like Brazil or Italy, where women's matches are considered by the soccer elite to be a minor annoyance or a curious complement to the "men's" game, but that attitude is changing. In Norway, soccer is the number one women's sport in terms of number of players, and youth schemes for girls between 7 and 19 years, involving some 4,000 teams, have been in existence for several years: this in a country with only four million inhabitants. In Germany there are more than 50,000 registered players and 1,250 women referees. In Nigeria, the First Lady, Ms. Babangita, has sponsored the national team with a personal financial contribution. In China, the women's national teams' successes far exceed the men's teams' on the world stage. In response, FIFA increased the number of teams allowed to participate in the 1999 World Cup from 12 to 16.

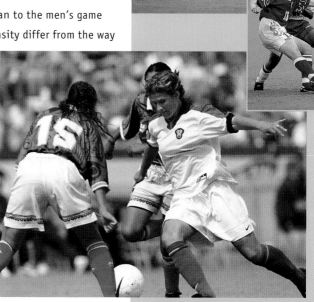

In 1994 the United States formed the W-League to foster the club game. The league split into two divisions in 1998, with a total of 33 teams. But U.S. schools are leading the revolution. A recent survey of *Sports Illustrated* showed that soccer is competing very effectively with football at the high school level, with interest for the latter declining in 37 of 50 states in the 1990s: as a result of direct pressure from kids graduating from youth leagues, more and more schools are dropping football in favor of soccer, which encourages the game for all players, male and female.

So while in several countries women's soccer is still struggling for life, in the U.S. it is trying to reinstate itself as the "real football," the game of choice for girls and boys. After all, this development might be considered evolutionary rather than revolutionary. For the game of football was so named in England and introduced to American schools. The U.S., it might be said, changed its name and its face—but not its soul. ∎

Elio Trifari is the Deputy Editor-in-Chief of La Gazzetta dello Sport; *published in Milan, the newspaper is the world's leading sports daily.*

Top: Japan's Maki Haneta shields the ball from Brazil's Pretinha in the 1996 Olympic Games. (Martin Venegas, Allsport) *Above middle:* Japan's Nami Ojoke struggles with Brazil's Roseli Belo in the 1996 Olympic Games. (Martin Venegas, Allsport) *Bottom:* Action from a Russia vs. Mexico game. (JBW/International Sports Images) *Below:* Australia's Linda Hughes controlling the ball. (JBW/International Sports Images) *Opposite:* Many European men's clubs also have women's teams; here Arsenal celebrates winning England's F.A. Cup. (Phil Cole, Allsport)

AT THE CROSSROADS: GEARING UP

BY DUNCAN IRVING

Several years ago, at one of the seemingly interminable World Cup draw ceremonies, FIFA General Secretary Sepp Blatter made an unwittingly prescient pronouncement. He of the mathematical esoterica and the endearingly mangled syntax, with which he explains the draw, took time out from his balls, brandy snifters, and baffling formulae to remark with a saucy glint in his eyes that "the future is feminine."

The reason behind this announcement was the arrival of a U.S. National Team star or two in a dress. In Blatter's eyes, they were a welcome change from the procession of

FOR THE FEMININE FUTURE

Fans at the 1995 FIFA Women's World Cup. (JBW/International Sports Images)

male soccer celebrities, many of whom were now broader of the beam and wider round the waist than they were at the peak of their powers. How times have changed. Blatter, of course, is FIFA's new president, while the U.S. women have gone from being a sporting novelty to household names in the canon of American soccer.

When the women won the inaugural World Championship in China in 1991, a handful of U.S. Soccer figures—men's coach Bora Milutinovic, general manager Bill Nuttall— showed up at JFK Airport to welcome the team home.

Now the team can't travel in peace. "Once the kids find out the team is showing up at, say Greensboro—they're there in numbers," says Head Coach Tony DiCicco. "And the exposure the National Team has had means that the players are all household names in a soccer family."

Talk of household names, endorsements, and book deals would have been unheard of a few years ago, let alone when U.S. Soccer launched its women's program in 1985. Mike Ryan, a Seattle-based coach, took the first squad of players to a tournament in Jesolo, Italy. The trip was not an unqualified success: the U.S. lost three of the four games in the tournament, but it did unearth one major talent in Michelle Akers.

U.S. coach Tony DiCicco has said, "Soccer is now so ingrained in society. Back when I started coaching women eight years ago, it was still a relatively new phenomenon. I'm not sure what our numbers were nationally then, but 30 percent were female; now it's 44 percent." Youth leagues and collegiate leagues have created a structure which allows players of all ages to develop their talent, making the U.S. number one in women's soccer. (All photos JBW/International Sports Images, except second from left, Allsport)

"It was laughable—we kind of just got sent to Italy for this tournament with some second-hand uniforms and no time to prepare or play together," said Akers. "We had one tournament or camp a year from 1985 to 1988. For a national team program, that's pretty pathetic. That first year, I didn't really understand what a national team was. I didn't grow up watching my national team play. I didn't really know about World Cup and what playing for a national team meant, or what goes along with it. I was just on this select team to go overseas and play soccer." She added, "When Anson came on board the next year, he pretty much wiped out the team." Out went Ryan and his Seattlites. In came the stars of Anson Dorrance's program at the University of North Carolina. "When Anson got on board, it became a lot more serious," said Akers. "He required that we

had more preparation." But the travel time together and tournament play were extremely limited. "Anson is huge. He is part of the legend in the development of women's soccer throughout the world. He helped set the standard that we have now. He taught us to be coaches, he taught us the responsibility of selling the game, and about our opportunities—if we do it right." Doing it right meant winning the Women's World Championship in China in 1991. The U.S. cumulatively blitzed its opposition 49–0 in CONCACAF qualifying, and the goals flew in throughout the tournament. Yet, the final against Norway was a tense affair. Still, the U.S. deservedly won 2–1 in front of 65,000 fans before returning to Bora, Bill, and a largely indifferent public. "There wasn't any money to cash in on from sponsors," said U.S. Soccer Secretary General Hank Steinbrecher. "We were very lucky to get our team together and get our team over there on very scant resources [about $175,000]."

After China, the team more or less disbanded. There were no sponsor dollars to fund the squad, competition was still scarce, and there were four years to kill before the U.S. defended the World Championship in Sweden. "Look, in 1992, the year after our win in China, we played like two games in Norway, with basically a youth team plus Mia Hamm," said DiCicco. "And 1993 was fairly inactive, too. At that point we were no longer the best team in the world. Somewhere in there we lost that. Losing to Norway drove that point home."

In 1994 DiCicco, after three years as assistant coach, took over from Dorrance. A year later, the team headed for Sweden. Wins over Denmark, Australia, and Japan placed the U.S. in the semifinal against Norway—a match the U.S. lost 1–0. "Losing in 1995 to Norway was a tremendous disappointment," said DiCicco. "About the only positive that I can take away from that loss was that Norway was the better team. That has been a great motivation for us because I think we had become a bit soft. The responsibility for that lay with everyone—the coaches, the players, and the program." Third place condemned the Americans to the ranks of the also-rans. But the chance for revenge was little more than a year away, at the Olympic Games. A 2–1 overtime win over Norway in the semifinals

put the U.S. in the final against China. Shannon MacMillan and Tiffeny Milbrett scored the goals in front of 76,489 delighted fans at Sanford Stadium in Athens, Georgia. The U.S. took the gold medal and made front-page news across the nation. Had NBC deigned to broadcast the game, more people would have witnessed the achievement. "The Olympics did a tremendous amount of good for heightening the awareness of the sport in this country," said Steinbrecher, "even though NBC at the time stood for No Bloody Coverage." The endorsements followed: Mia Hamm was singled out by advertisers as "The One" and promptly snagged an endorsement for Pert shampoo, before joining the ranks of *People* magazine's most beautiful people. U.S. Soccer's deal with Nike has ensured sufficient financial support for the national team program, as well as the development of national youth team programs.

And the women's game is no longer short of nationwide talent. One renowned coach remarked some years ago that there were 15 good players nationwide and 10 of them played

The University of North Carolina coach, Anson Dorrance, started the soccer program in 1979. His teams have won 15 out of 20 NCAA tournaments and produced such players as: Mia Hamm (left), Kristine Lilly, Carla Overbeck, Tisha Venturini, Tiffany Roberts, and Cindy Parlow (above). As UNC's famed basketball coach Dean Smith once said, "The University of North Carolina is a women's soccer school."

at North Carolina. Thanks to the passage of Title IX, the number of soccer players heading to college programs has risen dramatically.

"It's taken almost a generation for Title IX to have a real impact, from when I first started teaching in 1972 or 1973," said DiCicco. "Now we're seeing the fruits of that. There are many more good- to average-level players in college and coming through the ranks than before. And that tends to give the boost to make the best players better." While Title IX is widely considered a good thing—how could it be otherwise—it has been suggested that the younger players may be lacking the pioneer spirit of their predecessors.

"I think there's a difference," said Akers. "I look back and I think that the game was played more on guts than skill. There's better coaching, the athletes are fitter, they're technically better. In the heart department, I'm not sure they're of the same quality as those earlier players. Don't get me wrong, Title IX has done a lot for women's soccer. It has enabled them to get into the college ranks. They don't have to scratch their way into a program or create one of their own." However, the rest of the world is starting to want success badly, too. "Everybody expects the U.S. women's team just to show up on the field and win," said DiCicco. "But we know better. There are eight to ten teams capable of beating us on any given day. The gap between us and the other elite teams is decreasing. Brazil is the most improved of all of them."

Above: Trading cards of The U.S. National Team. Players have become idols for a generation of fans. "Look at someone like Mia Hamm," U.S. coach Tony DiCicco has said. "She's become a sports icon for women's athletics, not just women's soccer." (Allsport) *Opposite:* In 1998 the Florida Gators turned the Tar Heels head over heels to win the NCAA Championship. (JBW / International Sports Images)

In fact, managing expectations—from fans, sponsors, and U.S. Soccer's board—is one of Steinbrecher's current goals. "Everyone thinks we're going to waltz through World Cups and win," said Steinbrecher. "We have a very good team. But it should be about doing the best that we possibly can. Most of the time, one goal separates winning and losing a championship match. Anything can happen." To maximize the chances of success, U.S. Soccer earmarked some $3.2 million for the squad to prepare in 1999. The expenditure included a full-time training camp for the squad in Orlando, Florida. "I'm hoping that men's fans will grow to enjoy watching the women's game," said DiCicco. "You know, in tennis, I like to watch Pete Sampras, but I also enjoy watching Martina Hingis. That's the kind of level of acceptance I'd like us to reach." Added Steinbrecher, "I tend to agree with Blatter. The next hurdle for soccer around the world is getting women to play. And our country can lead the way." ■

Duncan Irving was a senior editor of Soccer America *magazine.*

TWO DAYS THAT CHANGED THE FACE OF WOMEN'S SPORTS

BY AARON HEIFETZ

The U.S. Women's Soccer team sweated and sacrificed in virtual anonymity for years before obtaining two incredible opportunities and succeeding like champions. Hundreds of games and thousands of practices preceded the magical summers in which the U.S. women captured gold in 1996 and the World Cup title in 1999.

U.S. forward Tiffeny Milbrett and defender Brandi Chastain did what every young female soccer player dreams of: they scored the winning goals for their country. For Milbrett, it was the gold-medal game of the 1996 Olympics. For Chastain, it was the historic fifth and final penalty kick in the 1999 Women's World Cup final. This is how they remember those momentous days.

TIFFENY MILLBRETT

YOU WOULD THINK we would have been nervous with 76,000 people in the stands and about to play for the first women's soccer Olympic gold medal, but we weren't. All the intimidation and jitters had already been played out in the semifinal against Norway, in front of about 65,000 fans.

It was very different preparing for the gold-medal game than for the semifinal. For the gold-medal game we were very loose and very confident. Everyone was like, "Gosh, we've come this far, all we have to do is play and the rest will take care if itself." Nobody doubted a thing.

The fans were absolutely fantastic. We could see everyone decked out in red, white, and blue with their faces painted and flags waving. I think everyone on our team was more awestruck than nervous at the whole thing.

We went ahead on a great goal by Shannon MacMillan in the first half, but China tied the score right before halftime. Still we felt no pressure. It was just one mistake, and a great player finished the chance on us. We just had to stay organized and not make any more mistakes.

The winning goal started with me camped out right at mid-field—I don't know why I was there. I started my run toward the penalty box. All the buildup took place on the right side, and the ball squeaked through to Joy Fawcett. From there, Joy did every-thing perfectly. If she would have released the ball a second earlier or a second later, it might not have been a goal. But she blew by the defense and passed it to me in the middle. I was wide open and just tapped it in. It's ironic that maybe my biggest goal might have been my easiest.

I came out of the game in the 69th minute, so I was sitting down at the final whistle when everyone exploded off the bench. If

Opposite: After winning the 1996 Olympic gold medal, Briana Scurry lifts the U.S. flag for 76,489 fans. *Below:* Tiffeny Milbrett in the 1996 Olympic Games final. *Following pages:* Glorious moments from the 1996 Olympic Games and the 1999 Women's World Cup. (All photos JBW/International Sports Images except second from right bottom row, Allsport.)

Right: A final 2–1 victory over China grants the U.S. the Olympic gold medal. (Allsport) *Opposite:* The U.S. women's team rejoices and hugs after Brandi's winning penalty kick in the Women's World Cup (JBW, International Sport Images)

you look at the tape, I didn't have any shoes on, but I didn't care. I jumped into the pile along with everyone else.

The most vivid and lasting memory is that the crowd stayed in the stands for the medal ceremony. They were just so excited, for the moment and for us. They came to see an historic event and that's what they got. People wanted to hold onto that as long as they could. We'll hold onto it forever.

BRANDI CHASTAIN

One strong image I have from the day of the World Cup final is riding on the bus into the Rose Bowl and seeing all the cars and the fans flowing into the stadium. The fact that the final was upon us really came into focus. When we saw all the American flags and all the people with their faces painted red, white, and blue, a wave of emotion hit us about how special the day was going to be.

Walking out into that stadium was similar to entering Stanford Stadium in Athens for the Olympic final in 1996. There was the noise factor; you not only could hear the fans, you could feel the noise. If you've ever been to the zoo when it's time to feed the lions and tigers, and they know it's time to eat, they roar so loud you can actually feel it in your body. It's like a rock concert, when the vibrations from the guitars run through you. The most surreal thing was that as soon as the opening whistle blew, you couldn't hear them anymore.

The game went on so long that it became evident one mistake or one really good play could decide the game. We talked to ourselves out on the field: "Just make this pass, just win this header. Get through this game." There was a keen sense that you didn't want to let your teammates down. It seemed the clock was moving so slowly during that 120 minutes. And then the penalty kicks came and went so fast that you couldn't believe the game was over.

Right after the final penalty was scored, it was amazing how you could hear the noise, because it was so quiet during the penalty kicks. It seemed that everyone in the stadium was holding their breath. I think I was too. After it was over, confetti filled the air and the energy in the stadium was like nothing we've ever experienced. The amazing thing was, as long as that 120 minutes was, the penalty kicks were done in a blink of an eye, before we could catch our breath. It's a journey that we'll remember for the rest of our lives. ■

Aaron Heifetz is the Press Officer for the U.S. Women's National Team.

THE WORLD IS WATCHING
THE U.S. NATIONAL TEAM
BY GRAHAME L. JONES

The U.S. Women's National Team training for the first Algarve Cup, in Portugal, in 1994. (Shaun Botterill, Allsport)

IT WAS A COOL NOVEMBER evening in 1991, and the 65,000 fans who gathered at Tianhe Stadium in Guangzhou, China, had come to see history being made. Down on the field, the national teams of Norway and the United States were engaged in a tense and dramatic struggle. At stake was nothing less than the first FIFA Women's World Championship, and the equally matched and determined teams wrestled for control of the game.

In the 20th minute, striker Michelle Akers crashed a header into the back of the Norwegian net to give the U.S. the lead. Eight minutes later, Linda Medalen tied it up with a looping header over the American goalkeeper. Halftime came and went, and as the minutes ticked by the battle grew even more intense. One mistake or one act of brilliance would decide it. Finally, with less than three minutes to play, Akers intercepted an errant back pass, touched the ball wide of Norway's onrushing goalkeeper, and then side-footed it into the open net. Goal!

A world championship had been won and the fireworks in the night sky over Guangzhou flickered and danced on the golden trophy that Akers and her beaming U.S. teammates held aloft in triumph.

Now flash forward four years. It is a sunny June afternoon in 1995, and the sellout crowd of 2,893 that has gathered at tiny Arosvallen Stadium in Vasteras, Sweden, has come to see the same teams meet in the second FIFA Women's World Championship. At stake is nothing less than a place in the final. In the 11th minute, Ann Kristin Aarones heads the ball into the net off a Gro Espeseth corner kick to give Norway a vital goal. For the next 79 minutes, the U.S. team pours heart and soul into the game, expending every ounce of energy and every bit of skill in a desperate attempt to break through the Norwegian defense and salvage the game. Shots crash against post and crossbar, shots are saved, shots fly agonizingly close, but it is not to be. A world championship has been lost, and this time there are tears. The team has settled for third place while Norway takes home the trophy after beating Germany in the final.

And now flash forward another four years. It is the eve of the third FIFA Women's World Championship, this one to be played in the United States, and the gleam of battle is once again in American eyes. What was won in 1991 and lost in 1995 must be reclaimed in 1999. At least that's Tony DiCicco's view. DiCicco, head coach of the U.S. team since 1994, led the team to the gold medal in the 1996 Olympic Games, defeating Norway in overtime, in a classic semifinal, and, beating China in the final. But despite that accomplishment, which made the U.S. women the first to win a world championship and the first to win an Olympic gold medal, DiCicco is intent on reclaiming the world title. "I don't think there's probably any other competition, maybe even the Olympics,

Below: In 1999, Kristine Lilly, "Queen of Cups," broke the all-time record in international appearances, male or female. "Through the 11 years on the National Team, every game has been a new lesson. People can tell you what to do and how to do it, but when you are on the field, you must make those decisions, and that experience is invaluable," said Kristine. *Opposite:* Tony DiCicco, seen here rallying the team during practice, has won 90 percent of his matches as the U.S. Women's National Team head coach. DiCicco has said, "It's important for the United States that this team has a legacy of being the best team ever." (All photos JBW / International Sports Images)

STARS
OF THE U.S. WOMEN'S NATIONAL TEAM

All photos JBW/International Sports Images except second row first from left, third row third from left and fourth row third from right, Allsport.

TISHA VENTURINI

BRIANA SCURRY

KRISTINE LILLY

MIA HAMM

DANIELLE FOTOPOULOS

JOY FAWCETT

SHANNON MACMILLAN

TIFFENY MILLBRETT

CARLA OVERBECK

CHRISTIE PEARCE

CINDY PARLOW

BRANDI CHASTAIN

SARA WHALEN

JULIE FOUDY

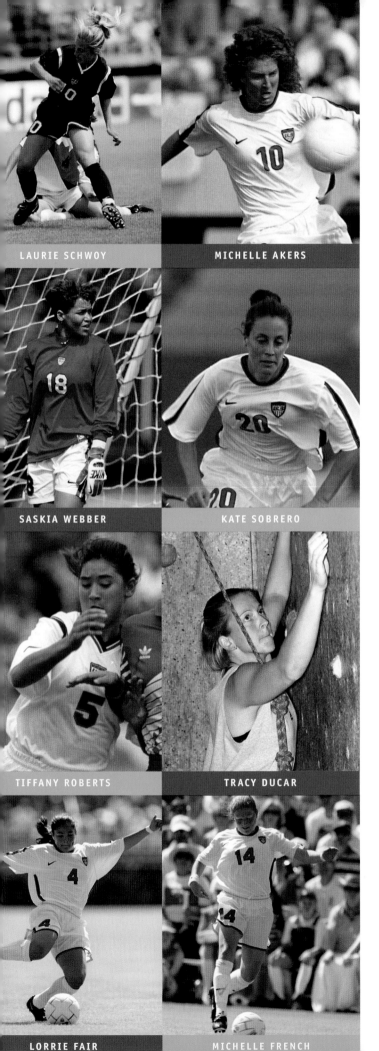

LAURIE SCHWOY

MICHELLE AKERS

SASKIA WEBBER

KATE SOBRERO

TIFFANY ROBERTS

TRACY DUCAR

LORRIE FAIR

MICHELLE FRENCH

that would have kept us together," he said in 1999. "We want to be World Champions again. Our goal was to be World Champions and Olympic champions together. We want to accomplish that now."

In 1999, the U.S. had one enormous advantage. Among the 26 players invited by DiCicco to residency camp in Florida before the 1999 World Cup there are no fewer than seven who were on the victorious 1991 and 1996 teams. Akers, of course, was one of them. So, too, were Kristine Lilly, Mia Hamm, Joy Fawcett, Carla Overbeck, Julie Foudy, and Brandi Chastain. The fact that these veterans are still able to hold their place in the starting lineup after a decade doesn't surprise DiCicco. "Some of these players have ten years on the National Team," he has said. "But the thing you've got to remember is that they were all teenagers when they started. The core of the team, in many ways, is not even 30. Some of them are just getting into their thirties. These are professional players who wanted to play at the highest level. If somebody played ten years in a top league, we probably wouldn't think much of it. But they haven't had a league to play in, so this is where they've been able to realize their competitive drives and dreams."

All of this means that there is an astonishing amount of experience built into the team. Couple that with talent and desire, and it makes the U.S. a formidable foe. DiCicco boasts about three of his many stars: "There's no replacement for Kristine [Lilly]," he said of the midfielder who has more national team appearances than anyone in history, male or female. "She's very versatile. She can play a lot of places, and she just makes the game happen wherever she is. Michelle [Akers] is another one. Who can dominate head balls like she can? Who can distribute the ball like she can? Who can still score goals? Who wants the responsibility in the semifinals of the Olympics, when you're down a goal, to take the penalty? Michelle is a champion, she's a winner, and she has unbelievable dedication to that. I don't know if there's a replacement for her. We might be able to get a *group* of players who can replace her."

Mia Hamm, who in 1998 became the first American and only the third player in the world to score 100 goals for her country, earns equal praise. "Everybody knows

Below: Michelle Akers displaying her strength in this confrontation with China's defender Yunjie Fan. (Doug Pensinger, Allsport) *Opposite:* Mia Hamm celebrates scoring her 100th goal in September 1998. (Ezra Shaw, Allsport)

her finishing is legendary, but her work defensively is just as good," DiCicco said. "What she's now started to do is she's started to take on the team. In other words, 'Get me the ball.' That's something she didn't do a few years ago."

Similarly irreplaceable, it would seem, are midfielders Foudy and Chastain, as well as defenders Overbeck and Fawcett. But the U.S. has had, for some time now, a wealth of talent clamoring for inclusion. No one could deny Olympic strikers Tiffeny Milbrett or Shannon MacMillan a place in the lineup, surely? Nor can gold medalists Tiffany Roberts or Tisha Venturini be excluded. Goalkeeper Briana Scurry is certainly a starter. The list goes on and on. Up-and-coming youngsters such as Kate Sobrero, Lorrie Fair, Cindy Parlow, Christie Pearce, Sara Whalen, and Danielle Fotopoulos are all in the hunt.

Considering the wealth and caliber of talent at their disposal, DiCicco and assistant coaches Lauren Gregg and Jay Hoffman might easily be regarded as superfluous. What can this array of stars possibly still have left to learn?

Quite a lot, as it turns out. "We do a lot of coaching," DiCicco said. "There are still so many little aspects of the game that we need to improve on—just the technical speed that we play at. We're still trying to get back some of the qualities that I thought were excellent in the Olympics. I think that comes from [being in] residency. Our long-ball service and the sharpness of our long-ball and our heading have gotten better this past year. There is still a lot of tactical stuff. As we get more sophisticated, there's another level to go to."

The U.S. veterans might be extraordinarily experienced—what other national team, male or female, can field *eight* players with more than 100 caps apiece?—but top international com-

petitors such as world champion Norway and runner-up Germany have highly competitive women's leagues where players hone their skills on a weekly basis. Such a league does not yet exist in the U.S., which is one reason why DiCicco would be hesitant to play, say, China or Sweden or Brazil with a lineup that does not include any of his 1991 or 1996 starters. "We would definitely be going in as the underdog," he said of such a scenario. "I think some of these younger players are farther along than they [the 1991 players] were at that age, and it's because of the total environment. There's better collegiate soccer and there's better coaching in the youth ranks. So the savvy kind of filters down from the total soccer experience, even from the men's side."

Several U.S. players moved abroad to play in professional leagues after the 1991 World Championship. Akers, for instance, went to Sweden, where in her 1992 season with Tyreso F.C. she finished as the top scorer in the nation, male or female. Foudy, Harvey, and Lilly also played in the Swedish women's league. Chastain, MacMillan, and Milbrett played in Japan. Eventually, they all came home. To its credit, U.S. Soccer recognized the players' competitive needs and responded by organizing more tournaments and hosting more foreign teams.

One result was the U.S. Women's Cup, which the Americans have hosted and won five years in a row. The number of games played by the National Team has increased substantially since the team was founded in 1985. In the first eight years of its existence, the U.S. played a total of 67 games. In the next six years, it played 120.

And 1998 was their best year yet. The U.S. finished 22-1-2, its only loss being to its strongest rival, Norway. One reason for such success—and perhaps a reason every bit as important as skill and experience—is the extraordinary closeness of the players. The U.S. is more than a team, it is a family, a description repeated by several players. There is remarkable camaraderie among them, a unity forged over the years through common purpose and mutual admiration. The players genuinely like each other and, having had no soccer heroines of their own to emulate, turn to each other for inspiration. If Akers can bend a ball into the net from 30 yards, Hamm wants to do the same. If Overbeck can slide-tackle the ball away from an opponent as clean as a whistle, Sobrero wants to do the same.

The younger generation of players—stars of the future such as Susan Bush and Lorrie has had a huge advantage in being able to grow up while watching players such as Milbrett and Fawcett lead the way. Now they, and others like them, are being integrated into the team and are learning that it is more than simply time spent together that builds U.S. unity. The all-for-one and one-for-all spirit that defines the U.S. team has not come about by accident.

"It comes down to the very basics," DiCicco explained. "If you see the equipment list for practice, you'll see Hamm's name up there, Akers' name up there, Foudy's name up there. We don't have a rookie responsible to handle those things, because we ought to do it together on the field and we ought to do it together on and off the field. "And that's the way they want it. Carla Overbeck doesn't want somebody else doing these jobs. She wants to be part of it. And when we're unloading a bus, you're going to see Carla and Lil [Lilly] and the veterans there first. So what we've built—not me personally, but as a team—is a culture.

The perfect team? Maybe. It's difficult to argue against two world championship, a gold medal, and a 15-year record of 144-31-12. Difficult, but not impossible. The rest of the world is catching up. "I hear that 'catching up' [phrase] all the time," DiCicco said, "and, yes, there is a portion of the world that is catching up, but it's not necessarily catching up to us. It's catching up to this elite group that we're part of."

"What we're gaining [in the women's game] is parity, and we need to have that. We need more teams being able to perform and beat teams. Since the Olympics we've seen Holland beat Germany, Australia beat China, Italy beat Norway, Brazil beat the U.S., France win the U-16 Nordic Cup. France is coming up, which isn't a surprise really. So when I hear 'catching up,' it's the rest of the world catching up to the elite group."

The U. S. played a bigger role in 1999. Regaining the world championship was the obvious goal, but beyond that there existed the opportunity for the players to use their talent and personality and overwhelming love for the game to raise women's soccer and women's sports in general to a higher plateau—not only in the U. S. but around the globe.

"I see women's soccer continuing to develop," DiCicco said. "I think we're going to see soccer much more engrained in society. I think it's going to be much more accepted as a spectator sport, even in the most macho societies. "People love to watch this team play and it's well-respected around the world, as some of these other teams are. We're winning people over."

DiCicco, of course, was won over long, long ago. "I have a tremendous respect for this team," he said. "It's an honor, an absolute honor, to coach them. It's a privilege. I think the world of them, not only as players but as people. I'm proud of them." ∎

Grahame L. Jones is the chief soccer writer for The Los Angeles Times *since 1973.*

women
AT WORK

SOCCER MOMS IN TRAINING

BY GLORIA AVERBUCH

I WAS JUST ANOTHER SOCCER MOM—lugging Gatorade and yelling from the sidelines—until I played the game.

I looked forward with excitement to my first parent versus child (soccer) match. Finally, I thought, a chance to truly share in my daughter's soccer experience. As we ran up and down the field, a group of rookie adults pitted against top-flight ten year olds, I was filled with confidence. "I can do this," I said to myself naively. In an instant, my illusions were shattered. For sailing high in the air, and right toward me, came that most coveted object: the ball.

Like a good student taking a final exam, all the right phrases went through my head: settle the ball, look up, make a pass. But as quick as those bookish lessons dutifully came to mind, they evaporated, replaced by a sense of utter panic. As I stared at the ball making its inevitable fall to earth, out of the corner of my eye I could (also) see the advancing army racing towards me. It included my own daughter, with a look in her eye of a predatory animal, usually reserved for league play. I tried to get a body part—any body part—on the ball, in order to clear it away. Anything to send the swarm of players somewhere else. During a few rest breaks, I resumed my sideline cheering (I was secretly relieved when a substitute took my place). Somehow I survived the rest of the match. Despite the physical fitness I possessed, I woke up the next day bruised and sore. I felt like the Tin Man in *The Wizard of Oz* before he found the oil can.

That game, in all of its detail (I can even remember the logo on the ball as it sailed toward me), is an experience I have not forgotten. It made me a different soccer mom, one with a heightened respect for young players. I applaud their bravery. I can see their efforts and accomplishments through new eyes. There was no experience like the real one to give me that vision.

When I was growing up, athletic girls were rare. They were rebels, labeled "tomboys"—as if playing sports somehow warranted a separate identity (and a questionable one at that)—and outside the norm. But the quest for equal rights for women helped turn the tide. Girls who play sports, and soccer in particular, have no special names now.

When you hear the term "soccer moms," you may think of women in ill-fitting sweatsuits, with no understanding of athletic efforts. But that isn't always true. We are more than our children's cheering fans. We are passionate—living vicariously through the athletic journey of our children. We cheer for them but at the same time envision what it would have been like for us. We are both pushed and pulled, rejoicing for the spunk and skill our daughters develop through this game, but mourning the lost opportunity to play ourselves. Some of us have been there, fleetingly, as marathoners or tennis players. Some, yes, have even begun to play the game.

Soccer Moms in Training began in Montclair, New Jersey, in the fall of 1998 when one mom on the sidelines returned a loose ball to her child's coach, a former player himself. "Nice pass," he said. "Too bad you don't play." "Too bad," she replied, "there's no soccer league for mothers." It was the beginning of a specially designed course for a group of soccer

As these youths in a Texas league demonstrate, soccer has become enormously popular among girls with 7.2 million participants and growing in 1998. Girls who play soccer are no longer outside the norm. They *are* the norm. One of the events that made this possible was the passage of Title IX in 1972 (symbolically, the year Mia Hamm was born), the portion of the education amendment that prohibits sex descrimination in educational institutions that receive any federal funds. This has immeasurably improved women's sports opportunities. (Phil Stevens)

Previous page: Six year olds—the age at which players can begin organized soccer—struggle to maintain possession of the ball. (Bild Byran) *Below:* Seven- and eight-year-old girls gather for a cheer before a game. (Bild Byran) *Opposite:* A dad takes on the difficult task of consoling his daughter after a loss. (Bild Byran)

moms to learn to play the game. Every session—dressed in pinnies and cleats—they sweat, they struggle, they get better, and they learn about the game, as well as how to play it. They proclaim with amazement how much more they understand their children's efforts and how much they respect the challenges young players face.

Soccer begins with small steps, ones players can take with their moms in order to share their soccer experience. We just need them to invite us, to encourage us. How about a little backyard passing? We'll catch or fetch the ball, even try back-and-forth headers. Many of us are willing to give it a go, even just for the opportunity to become closer to our children. Who's to say moms can't learn the game from their offspring? They can become our mentors. Teaching us what they have learned also hones their own skills.

Playing the game, though, will not make us equals or change our roles. Nor should it. We cherish those roles, for many reasons. As soccer moms, we are a special breed—well-versed in folding chairs and how to dress in layers against the cold. We take pride in our spectating expertise. Yet despite our joy at watching our children, we find ourselves in an odd situation. We automatically rise to the level of emotion of our players, feeling the nervous excitement for the battle to be waged on the game field. As our children suit up in their uniforms and fill their water bottles, our adrenaline, too, gets pumped. Yet theirs is a contest we cannot enter. Our children bring their emotional preparation to its logical conclusion: they play the game. We are relegated to the sidelines. It's no wonder our cheering becomes so passionate, our emotions sometimes out of control. Where else are our feelings to go?

These deep and powerful feelings—and what arises from them—are what we share with our

children. As parents, we do our best to help our children. And they, in turn, can help us—by understanding our role, and guiding us in the challenges we face to learn how best to support them in their efforts. We need to take it easy. One too many sore throats from sideline yelling at games eventually teaches us. Moms must face each soccer experience by looking always toward the horizon. One practice, one game—no matter what game—is merely a blip on the radar screen of our children's career. We must pace ourselves. If our children keep at it during our entire nurturing tenure, 18 years is a long time to yell.

While we're at it, my daughters say, let's change the traditional roles. "Why do the moms always plan the team parties?" they ask. If they could remake the parent part of youth soccer, they'd switch the roles: more moms would volunteer to coach; more dads would bring the drinks and cut up the oranges; moms would stick in the corner flags and run the lines; moms and dads would both attend games. My 12 year old's final piece of advice to players: when you grow up, get involved with your children. Change the old ways.

There will always be a place for the traditional role of soccer mom. Bringing the orange slices is still important. Being there for our children—in every way—is part of the unconditional love we feel for them. And players can (begin to) repay their moms, simply by hugging us back, and saying, "Thank you." ■

Gloria Averbuch is the author, with Ashley Michael Hammond, of Goal! The Ultimate Guide for Soccer Moms and Dads *(Rodale Press, 1999). Averbuch, a competitive masters runner, is the mother of two top-level soccer players: 12-year-old Yael and 9-year-old Shira.*

ADVICE FROM TWO DAUGHTERS: WHAT SOCCER MOMS **SHOULD** AND SHOULDN'T DO!

DOS

- Get your player to practices and games on time. Nothing is worse than sprinting to join the group with shinguards flapping.
- Attend and pay attention to the games. Playing is tiring enough without having to recite what happened.
- Learn the right terms. Scoring is called a goal, not a touchdown.
- Know what position(s) your child plays. Use word association if necessary (i.e., forward=front; wing=sides).
- Learn what offsides is. Break with tradition and be the only parent NOT to ask, "What's that?"
- Know that not every time your player goes down, she was fouled. Your perfect child can fall on her own, too.
- Cheer encouragement; don't try to coach. "Way to go," is definitely better than, "Get the ball."
- Take an interest; ask her to show you what she's learned. (Don't worry; she's highly unlikely to challenge you to a one-on-one in order to demonstrate).
- Allow her to take risks. "Sweetie, don't get too close to those big, bad defenders," is not exactly useful advice.
- Bring your credit card to tournaments; employ your shopping skills.

DON'TS

- Don't kiss your child good luck in front of her teammates if she is over age 5.
- Don't knit or pass the time gossiping during her game. That afghan for your niece can wait.
- Don't run out onto the field if she goes down, unless you've watched every episode of "E.R."
- Don't cringe when you hear the crack of shinguards. They're meant to last.
- Don't brag about your child (especially to the coach). Every parent thinks her daughter is the next Mia Hamm.
- Don't tell her she looks pretty in her uniform.
- Don't argue with the ref (at least not so he or she can hear).
- Don't offer cookies to the ref (cash works better).
- Don't yell "Boot it!" "Shoot it!" "Pass it!" etc.—("You go girl," will do).

REAL SOCCER MOM
CARLA OVERBECK: MOTHER OF ONE, CAPTAIN OF ELEVEN

BY JOHN POLIS

SHE IS A PREMIER ATHLETE. An Olympic gold-medal winner. One of the most consistent players ever to compete in international women's soccer.

She has the work ethic of a champion, has received many awards, and been praised by sportswriters around the world. They call her "world champion," "inspirational leader," and the "heart and soul" of the U.S. defense. But of all the titles and honors bestowed upon Carla Overbeck, captain of the U.S. Women's National Soccer Team, the title that means the most to her is "mom."

In the country that invented the term "soccer mom," Overbeck takes the definition to a new level by carefully balancing her roles as professional athlete, wife, and mother. No babysitters here—Overbeck's baby goes right along to practice with Mom.

Young son, Jackson, born in 1997, has been attending soccer workouts with his mom since even before he was born. The mother-to-be maintained her fitness by training right up until two months before she had the baby. Three days after Jackson was born, she went right back to work as assistant coach of the Duke University women's team, but despite her drive to maintain her performances as one of the best woman soccer players in the world, this soccer mom—when push comes to shove—puts the mom part before soccer.

"Before you have a child, you think all of these things are important: your job, winning and losing games," she told *Dallas Morning News* writer Thomas Huang. "Now nothing is as important as that kid."

"I think we as females in America are fortunate," Overbeck has said. "A lot of time in other countries their societies don't accept women playing sports. That's one of the reasons we are successful, because our society is very accepting of it."

Women soccer players in the U.S. also benefit from the momentum established by political legislation that ensures equal budgets for both men's and women's intercollegiate soccer teams. And the decision-makers at U.S. Soccer have (almost overnight, it seems) seen the U.S. Women's National Team vault to a position of world leadership, while the men's team, despite three consecutive appearances in the World Cup, still struggles for respect.

Below: Thirty-two-year-old Joy Fawcett is a veteran defender on the U.S. Women's National Team. Here she awaits a congratulatory hug from her number one fan, her daughter Katey. *Opposite:* Carla Overbeck with Jackson at the 1998 Goodwill Games celebration. (All photos JBW/International Sports Images)

Overbeck has played in 63 consecutive international games—a record for an American woman—which includes a streak of 3,547 consecutive minutes against 19 different national teams. That streak, which began on August 4, 1993, might still be going were it not for the fact that she took a year off so that she and her husband, Greg, could have Jackson, born in August 1997. (JBW/International Sports Images)

Scoring goals by the bucketful, the U.S. women usually dominate their opponents. Such success spawns reams of publicity on players, with most of it going to those who score the goals. Thus, Overbeck's critical role for the U.S. has been overshadowed by the goal-scoring of Michelle Akers or the explosive emergence of Mia Hamm (the heir to Akers' goal-scoring legacy). But make no mistake about it. Carla Overbeck is a big-time star.

If she were a man, the international journalists, broadcasters, and pundits would mention her name in the same breath with the great defenders who played the game—Brazil's Alberto, England's Moore, Italy's Baresi, and Germany's Beckenbauer. For she has much in common with these great players, not the least of which are qualities that coaches look for in an outstanding defensive leader: the ability to organize the defense, to read the game, to support teammates with defensive cover, and to start the attack with a thoughtful, well-placed pass.

Entering her 12th year as the bulwark of the U.S. Women's National Team, the 31-year-old Overbeck is a rock-steady team captain who quietly goes about her business without the fanfare and publicity that surrounds her teammates.

Carla Werden, who started playing for the Dallas Sting club at age 11, is part of a generation of young Americans who adopted soccer as its game. An all-around athlete, she played both volleyball and basketball at Richardson High School. In soccer, she played with the Sting all the way up to the U-19 age bracket. Then one day Anson Dorrance, coach of the University of North Carolina women's team, saw her play. "I liked Carla the first time I saw her play with the Dallas Sting," said Dorrance, who was Carla's regional select team coach. "She was a play-making midfielder, but I saw her as a sweeper back in a man-marking system and that's the way we used her at Carolina." At Carolina, she was part of four national championship teams coached by Dorrance, as well as a three-time collegiate All-American.

"One of the things I like most about her was her leadership quality, which is evident when you watch her play. I always tell my players there are two ways to win. The first is the get-out-of-my-way Mia Hamm/Michael Jordan approach, while with the second approach, you lead by example and motivate those around to victory. In practice games, Carla would always organize her team to victory."

So good was Werden at reading the situation within a game that, Dorrance says, she is the only player he has ever had who calls out needed substitutions from the field. "She would shout out that so-and-so should be taken out now," Dorrance recalled. "I respected her so

much—and she was so right—that whenever she had a top-of-the-lung substitution, I would warm someone up immediately."

Behind what can be a stern exterior on the field, Werden exhibits a warmth that endears her to her teammates. "At the airport, she is the first one to start slinging luggage. She is a kind, selfless person who operates without any ego. Her achievements may be legendary, but she doesn't carry herself that way."

She helped lead the U.S. to its first great victory in international soccer at the first FIFA World Championship for Women's Football in China in 1991. The U.S. women, with Dorrance at the helm, made a bold statement by winning six consecutive games on the way to the championship. She choreographed a defensive back line—Joy Biefeld (Fawcett), Linda Hamilton, and Debbie Belkin—which allowed only five goals in six games. In all of 1991, the Werden-led U.S. National Team defense gave up just 22 goals in 28 games, compiling a 21-6-1 record.

"There's no question she ran the show for us," Dorrance adds. "Biefeld was a former midfielder. Hamilton didn't have the national team experience. And Mary Harvey, our goalkeeper, wasn't that experienced. It was Carla who took a patchwork defense and turned it into a formidable force."

"DON'T JUST CHEER YOUR OWN CHILD. IT'S A TEAM."

So what does the Mother of All Soccer Moms want for her son?

"Certainly I would want him to play sports, but I also want him to learn to play the piano, to do a lot of things. I think sports are a great thing for kids, it's healthy, and a lot of times it keeps them out of trouble."

But, Overbeck cautions, sports should be a choice that the youngster makes and not necessarily the parent. "Sports are not for everyone, so it's important that kids find something. Maybe painting or a musical instrument. If the parents force sports on them, then they will approach it with a negative attitude." And once the child is in sports, Carla thinks they should be supportive, but not intrusive. "Support your child, but support every other child out there as well," she implores. "You set an example as a parent when you are out there watching. Don't just cheer your own child. It's a team."

Would she coach Jackson? "I'd probably let some other parent do that," she says. "But I'll definitely be at the games, sitting in the stands—and not saying a word." Action speaks louder than words, and this soccer mom prefers to lead by setting an example of leadership and hard work.

Dorrance likes to tell the story when one day he interrupted one of his regular UNC team

training sessions after seeing Carla working out on her own. She was banging the ball off a wall, while baby Jackson watched patiently nearby. "I stopped practice and told my players to watch her," Dorrance recalls. "I told them that Carla is what a champion is all about. She didn't know we were watching her. But there she is, out there killing herself, with no support system, no coach—nothing driving her but her own indomitable will." ∎

John Polis was Director of Communication Services for the United States Soccer Federation. He is now an executive at the USISL, the U.S.'s largest soccer league.

NINETY MINUTES BEFORE KICKOFF

BY JOHN POLIS

NINETY MINUTES BEFORE KICKOFF, you can hear a pin drop in the locker room of the U.S. Women's National Team.

The game jerseys are ever-so-carefully draped—name side out—at each dressing cubicle. The locker room is stocked with tape, analgesic, nutritional bars, sports drinks, water, shoe polish, chewing gum, towels, and soap. The team's advance staff of equipment handlers and medical personnel, working in unfamiliar surroundings, scurry around to create a comfortable environment for the players.

On the bus trip to the stadium from the hotel, it's a mixed bag. Tiffany Roberts wears headphones, rap music pulsating. Joy Fawcett sits quietly, reading. Groups of players carry on conversations. Some players are singularly pensive, considering the upcoming game in thoughtful silence.

"Each player prepares for a game in a different way," says U.S. Assistant Coach Lauren Gregg. A coach with the team for more than ten years, she has been on the bench during the team's greatest triumphs—China in '91, Atlanta in '96, and the World Cup in '99. A former player, she is paid to know what makes her players tick. She observes, and offers help if needed. But when it comes to players' pregame routines, she just mostly stays out of their way.

"Well in advance of the game, we have talked to the players and asked them where they need to be in order to be fully prepared. We realize that people are different, and players prepare for a game in vastly different ways. We feel you have to honor that—unless, of course, the players are not performing."

The process becomes more structured as Game Day approaches. And while players are free to put their game faces on in whatever way they want, the team activities of game day comprise the only routine in the U.S. camp that remains—year-in and year-out—sacred.

After a big buffet breakfast in the hotel (around 9:30 a.m.), players report to a 15-minute meeting, which is called the Scouting Report. Coach Gregg, who spends months on the road each year scouting the team's international opponents, analyzes the opposing team. Sometimes she will choose three opposing players and discuss their tendencies in detail. She might diagram a few of the opponent's set plays or show a few minutes of video to reinforce a key point.

"We want our players to be at a very comfortable place with regard to knowing what to expect from the other team," she says. "We don't overdo it. Less is more. We try to show how the opponent might be vulnerable. While we do focus on the other team, we are really studying them to learn more about ourselves, and what we must do to be successful."

In the late morning and early afternoon, Head Coach Tony DiCicco holds individual meetings, lasting only one to five minutes, with certain players. "He'll ask a player if she has any questions about what the team needs from her today," says Gregg. "Sometimes, he might not even talk with a player about soccer. It might be just to see how they feel with respect to an injury."

The pregame meal is held at 3:30 p.m. This is a fairly large meal followed by quiet time,

Few 21-year-old players can summon as much big match experience as Cindy Parlow: 42 international appearances and 17 goals. With the University of North Carolina Tar Heels she has won one NCAA tournament and placed second in 1998 to the Florida Gators. (JBW / International Sports Images)

when players can relax in their rooms, sleep, watch TV, or do whatever they feel like doing. "The time before we go out and warm up is very much individual," says Gregg. "This is when I try to watch the players and observe their moods. I might walk around and talk to players, give them some one-on-one time. And sometimes I won't talk with anyone. It just depends."

Then it's 6 p.m. and time for the Pregame Meeting in the locker room. Three large sheets of poster paper are taped to the locker room wall. They list the team lineup, along with diagrams and positioning notes on restarts, penalty kicks, free kicks inside and outside of shooting range, and corner kicks (who takes them). The players have already studied their game strategies and know who is playing, but the team lineup posted on the wall has become a tradition.

"We review the offensive and defensive keys to the game—usually three each," says Gregg. "We revisit every detail to make sure everyone is on the same page. Experience tells us that correct or incorrect execution can win or lose a game. Take defensive corner kicks, for example. To make sure everyone has it right, we sometimes walk through our position assignments right there in the locker room."

The team's structured, 25-minute warm-up period consists of a mixture of stretching, light running, shooting, and ball work. "Some of our warm-up routine has been here for ten years or more," says Gregg. Returning to the locker room, they change from warm-up shirts to full game uniform. Some grab something to eat or drink. Others head for a last bathroom pit stop. DiCicco has one final team get-together. Co-captains Julie Foudy and Carla Overbeck call the players together on their own for a final word. Minutes later the players enter the field for pregame introductions.

"Someone told us a story about when Abraham Lincoln was given eight hours to chop down a tree; he spent six hours sharpening his ax. That describes our program perfectly. It's about putting things in place. Every detail could be the margin of victory, and we attend to every last detail."

And then there's that important intangible that ties it all together—team chemistry. And, as Gregg points out, it's not something that starts by osmosis. "It's something we teach. Something that is worked on by each player. Once everyone buys in, you have a chance for success. Team chemistry enables a team to summon up the courage and fortitude to reach the next level under difficult circumstances."

"When we played Norway in the Olympic semifinal game, the game was so difficult, so taxing, that the players gave everything they had and left it all out on the field. But the next day, we had to think about the gold-medal game. We had to find the next level—individually and collectively."

Finding that next level is a never-ending process. Once the game is over, the preparation cycle of the U.S. team begins all over again. There is no rest for a champion, says Gregg. "Once it was thought that no one could run a four-minute mile. Now it is commonplace. People also used to think that women couldn't play soccer at a high level. Now that the U.S. team has set the highest standard in women's soccer, other teams are out there gunning for us." ■

Above: Assistant Coach Lauren Gregg (in black) watches the team warm up. *Below:* Practice balls ready to be used. *Bottom:* Many on the U.S. team have the added experience helping others prepare for big games: Mia Hamm was U.N.C.'s Assistant Coach in 1998. (All photos Pam / International Sports Images)

CHANGING THE WORLD
JULIE FOUDY: COMMENTATOR, PIONEER

BY GRAHAME L. JONES

IT WAS BITTERLY COLD that December afternoon in the central California town of Fresno. So cold that the several thousand fans present at Bulldog Stadium on the Fresno State University campus were bundled in coats, scarves, hats, and gloves. All they could talk about was how it had snowed in town that morning for the first time in decades. Twenty-eight minutes into the U.S.'s game against Ukraine, however, the bleak weather was forgotten. Defender Kate Sobrero collected the ball and, from the halfway line, threaded a pass through to Julie Foudy. The midfielder sprinted forward, wrong-footed one defender with a deft touch, and outpaced two others. She looked up and then unleashed a fierce, 20-yard shot that flew past the diving goalkeeper and caromed into the back of the net off the right post.

Goal! Foudy's 25th in a decade of international play. She beamed, thrust her right arm into the air, forefinger extended, and was immediately enveloped by teammates.

If any player on the U.S. team typifies what her close friend and co-captain Carla Overbeck calls "the will to win," it is the 29-year-old world champion and reigning Olympic gold medalist. There are only nine players in the world who can claim those twin honors and seven of them are still active on the U.S. team. But it is more than medals that binds the American squad together, more than on-field success that makes it not only the most tight-knit of teams, but an example for all of women's sports.

The funny thing is, the players do not talk much about their position as role models or about how they are "empowering"—to use a '90s buzz word—the next generation of female athletes. Instead, they lead by example, and no one more so than Foudy. "Every single woman on this team is very independent and very confident. That's just who you are."

The intangibles that Foudy has gained as an athlete are more valuable than all the honors won and all the places seen. "Women who are involved in sports, studies show, have a lot more self-esteem and confidence," she says. "You can see it with the players on our team."

"I think sports empower you. There are so many positives behind it. You have to learn to adapt to different things, on and off the field. There are a lot of different pressure situations. There's how you deal with them and, most important, how you deal with a team environment. We're all individuals on the team, but it doesn't work unless we can pull it all together."

If three words could sum up the U.S. team, they would be these: competitive, confident, and caring. Foudy typifies all three.

"I'm very competitive in everything, not just sports," she said. "But I'm not a mean competitor. I remember as a kid I was always very competitive about my schoolwork, my grades, and just making a difference in life in general. After I'm done with soccer, I don't want to just have a job that's nine to five and not really be doing anything to make a difference."

Making a difference is especially important to the U.S. women's team, which is why they

Above: Midfielder Julie Foudy in the 1996 Olympic Games final. (JBW/International Sports Images) *Following pages:* Julie fights for the ball against Brazil. (JBW/International Sports Images)

"SPORTS EMPOWER YOU. YOU HAVE TO LEARN TO ADAPT TO DIFFERENT THINGS."

involve themselves in antismoking campaigns, efforts against drunk driving, the eradication of child labor, and other social issues. Foudy was featured in newspaper stories across the U.S. after she visited Pakistan at the invitation of Reebok to see firsthand the moves the sports equipment company is making there to do away with child labor in the manufacture of soccer balls. "The good thing about that was that it at least brought some type of spotlight to that issue," she said. "We're not going to make huge strides overnight, but I would love to stay involved in that issue. . . I think you'll see that a lot of players, postcareer, will be more expressive about things like that."

There is no ego on the U.S. team. The players aren't like so many athletes today who regard astronomic salaries and fawning fans as their rightful due. They play for the love of the game, for the camaraderie, for the simple joy of being on such a team, of being the best. Was the self-assurance always there, Foudy was asked, or did it develop gradually? "I think it's half and half," she said. "It's kind of the big battle between nature versus nurturing. I think a lot of it stems from your family. There's a lot of good family blood on our team. I think also it comes with playing at the highest level. It's not an overconfidence, though. That's what I love about this team. It's the confidence of, 'I've been training against the best players in the world.' And once you convince yourself that, 'Yes, I belong in this group as a player,' then that only builds on what confidence you already have."

Now a new generation of national team stars is being developed for the future. Outstanding young players such as Susan Bush and Michelle French are being integrated into the squad and the confidence needs to be passed along and shared. "That's all the more important now," Foudy said, "because the younger kids coming in have grown up watching Mia (Hamm), Kristine (Lilly), Carla (Overbeck), Michelle (Akers), and everyone, which we didn't have. So they're even that much more intimidated coming in. So the first thing we do is try to build confidence."

Foudy did not have such soccer role models as a youngster. But neither were many limits imposed on her. She has played the game since she was seven years old. Now she coaches kids in soccer camps and can tell the impact the U.S. team is having on tomorrow's players. "They always think you're like this superwoman type of figure that they see on TV," she said, "and then when they see you in real life it's like, 'Oh, I can do that. I can do the Olympic Development Program. I did the same thing she did.'"

Foudy's own dreams carried her to Stanford University, where she won All-American honors, earned her degree in biology, and was offered a scholarship to medical school. Instead, she decided to pursue a television career and already has the 1998 World Cup experience on her resume. All the while she played on the national team, first being called up in 1987 at age 16, making her debut the following year at 17, and holding a starting role ever since. It was not until she went overseas, she said, that she came across discrimination against the very idea of females being able to play soccer: "When I was growing up playing soccer and other sports, I never once came across any type of gender bias." But while studying in Spain she remembers how she and some women friends tried to join male players in practice and the reaction that that provoked. "They would just freak out," she said. "Literally it just shocked them that we could play. I'd always heard about that, that women didn't play the sport in [some] other countries, but to see the look on their faces, the genuine shock. It was weird because you never came across that in America."

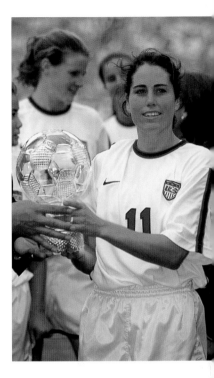

"I have a British husband, and even his parents still can't grasp how it's so different [in the U.S.], how everyone here plays," remarked Foudy. "It's not girls, it's not boys, it's everyone. My mother-in-law will still be like, '. . . and *you* hit it with your head?'" Foudy drops the fake English accent, laughs, and then recalls Brazil. There, fans in the stands hurled insults at the U.S. women players when they first visited. Now, Brazil is changing. Now its women's team is becoming a source of pride. There is no question that Foudy and company helped alter the South American fans' perspective with their play and their professionalism.

Slowly, the bias against women in sports is being eradicated. It won't happen overnight, and it won't happen everywhere, but progress is being made. "Eventually it's going to change," Foudy said. "It already has. Changing attitudes take a long time. England's the same way. I think that's why the United States has been so successful in women's sports, because it gives women that empowerment."

Soccer is a contact sport. At its highest level, the intensity is keen. That applies to women as much as it does to men. But there is a difference. "We're pretty aggressive, but I think we're probably less aggressive than men," Foudy said. "I mean, obviously there's a physical side to the game, but it's frowned upon to be overly aggressive. The intensity is the same, but the physical side isn't necessarily the same. Like I watched Italy versus England in a 1998 World Cup qualifier on television and it was just bone-breaking tackles on every play. Scary. I was thinking, 'Sheesh! I wouldn't want the ball. These guys are coming in so hard, studs-up, both feet, every play.' You don't see that in the women's game."

In Fresno, on that cold December day, Foudy scored her first career hat trick in a 5–0 victory. Her second goal came in 51 minutes into the game, when she snuck in at the back post and knocked in a cross from Lilly at close range. Her third came two minutes later, a long-range rocket like the first, this time off a pass from Tisha Venturini. Her delight in the goals was evident, but weeks later she still was unable to explain their origin. "I don't know," she said, laughing. "I think it was the donuts and beer I had for breakfast. Did you see my look of shock every time I scored?" Though shocked, she was able to enjoy the moment and then to put on a headset and tell the television audience all about it. One of her comments is memorable: "I love it," she said of the team's new 4-3-3 formation that gives her the freedom to attack more. "I can take the ball and chain off my foot. I can get forward, finally."

In a sense, that is exactly what the U.S. players, the first world and first Olympic champions, have been doing these past ten years—unshackling the sport from the outdated ideas of the past and freeing the future for all women athletes. That, not the gold medals, will be their greatest accomplishment and their lasting legacy. ■

BRIANA SCURRY KEEPING THE GOAL

BY JOHN POLIS

(gol'ke'per) n. The player who defends the goal, as in soccer. Brash, cocky, often seen hollering instructions at teammates. Takes charge. Exhibits leadership qualities. Eccentric. Sometimes accused of not having both oars in the water.

BRIANA SCURRY HASN'T ALWAYS personified the role that most accurately mimics life's travails in the last line of defense.

Quite the opposite. In high school and college she quietly went about her business, waiting patiently for the moment to summon those marvelous athletic skills and make an acrobatic save. Content to let others do the talking, she paid a price by enduring the physical pounding resulting from having to make 20 to 25 saves per game.

All that changed in 1994, when she came to the U.S. Women's National Team to work with Head Coach Tony DiCicco. A former goalkeeper, the coach knew he wouldn't have to deal with the qualities often attributed to goalkeepers: great athletes with flaky, off-the-wall mentalities spilling over into life off the field.

Scurry was none of that. Yet, through hard work and a determination by Scurry to improve, DiCicco not only got his new recruit talking like a goalkeeper, but communicating like a leader. As a result, Scurry has her international career in full bloom. She was the USA's starting goalkeeper in the 1995 Women's World Cup in Sweden. She was between the posts a year later during the Americans' dramatic gold-medal victory in the Olympic Games in Atlanta. She is the complete player, augmenting her athletic skills with a new-found ability to inspire those around her.

"It's common for goalkeepers to yell at defenders when they make a mistake," said DiCicco. "But when the defenders in front of you do well, you have to wine and dine them a bit. Briana has had to learn that. She has learned to dismiss mistakes, stay calm, and get ready for the next play."

Briana Collette Scurry got her first big opportunity when DiCicco brought her into a training camp prior to a

1994 National Team trip to Portugal. Veteran Mary Harvey was out with a knee injury. Saskia Webber was the starter, but Scurry's performance in camp earned her a spot on the roster. She made her international debut on March 16, 1994, with a shutout against Portugal, and has been the USA starter ever since.

"That's not an easy thing to do—be our starting goalkeeper for five years," said DiCicco, who each year sees more top female goalkeepers coming up. "She has the best mental approach to the game of any goalkeeper I've coached. She's confident and competitive, but there is a calming side to her; she doesn't get caught up in the excitement of the moment. Just when panic would set in with some players, she seems able to detach herself."

DiCicco never saw Scurry play until her junior year in college, when she played for a regional team at a U.S. Soccer–sponsored festival in Massachusetts. "It was right after the world championship in China," DiCicco recalls, "and I had Mia Hamm and Mary Harvey as the only veterans in the camp. The rest were all young players. Briana was playing on one of the other amateur regional teams, and though she didn't play all that well, her great qualities were imbedded in my mind."

Scurry was a consensus choice as the nation's top female goalkeeper in 1993, as she helped lead the University of Massachusetts to a 17-3-3 record and the semifinals of the NCAA Division I women's tournament. She was selected for the All-American Second Team, the All-Northeast Region Team, and the All-New England Team. During her four years at UMass, she recorded 37 shutouts in 65 starts, with a 0.56 goals-against average. Fifteen of those shutouts were in her senior year (1993) where, in 23 games, she had a goals-against average of 0.48. She was an All-American in high school, leading Anoka (Minn.) Senior High School to the 1989 Minnesota prep championship. That same year she was voted the top female athlete in the state.

The U.S. coach said that Scurry and other members of the National Team have come back from a letdown

following the 1996 Olympics Games
"A lot of our players questioned
whether they wanted to do this for
another four years. I think Briana was at
a crossroads. I didn't take her on a trip to
Brazil in December 1997, and told her she
had to sort it out, to decide if soccer was
in her future. Then, in January 1998 I saw
a difference in her. She decided she wanted
to keep playing. Her discipline and openness
to training improved. I can see that she is having
fun playing again."

Watching Scurry in goal, the first thing you
notice is that she moves with speed, grace, and
an athletic flair that invites you to look forward
to the next time she will handle the ball. "She has
explosive athletic skills, in that she'll dive or get up
to the ball in a very short period of time," describes DiCicco. "She's very competitive. If the game requires her to take
a physical risk, then she's going to do it."

Beyond strength, beyond athletic ability, Scurry has a
cerebral quality about her that, according to DiCicco,
serves her well. "The new Briana is ready to make
the big play mentally—before she
has to do it physically," says DiCicco.

The new Briana also thinks about her career long
term—about how she influences the young people who
see her play. Realizing that being a professional athlete
includes off-the-field responsibilities, she is eager to do
all she can to positively influence kids' lives.

"I definitely see myself as a role model for African-
American kids, all kids," she told Charles F. Gardner of
The Milwaukee Journal Sentinel. "It's hard for little
African-American girls, in particular, because they see
Michael Jordan, they see the Mailman (Karl Malone), they
see Deion Sanders, and they're all men. And they're so far
out there that they can't reach them. They're like gods,
almost. When they see me out here . . . and women's

basketball
players at that
level, they see something
they can aspire to."

Scurry also recog-
nizes her unique posi-
tion as one of the few black females to play soccer for the
National Team. "I grew up in a predominantly white sub-
urb," she said in an interview with John Smallwood of *The
Philadelphia News.* "Whichever sport I played, I was pretty much the only black kid on the team. It never bothered
me because I was well-received by my teammates. . . . I
also thank my parents because they taught me to be well-
adjusted, view the situation around me, and be friends
with everyone regardless of color. But I am proud of my
heritage, and I take very seriously my role of showing
African-American youth, and people in general, that we
can excel in sport—or in anything." ■

MIA HAMM
GRATEFUL FOR HER GIFTS

BY BONNIE DE SIMONE

SHE HAS GIVEN HER SPORT A FACE.

A heart-shaped face.

A game face.

Mia Hamm has nothing left to prove, yet she plays on. She is only 28 years old. That's easy to forget, because she has always been there. Women's soccer, like a slow-motion film of a tulip opening, has bloomed out of adolescence into adulthood right along with her.

Hamm has helped win every title there is to win: in college, at the world level, at the Goodwill Games, in the Olympic Games. She will almost certainly finish her career as the world's all-time leading scorer, which is a bit like saying that Secretariat was a few lengths better than the other horses, or that Michael Jordan sure could jump. Hamm has set the bar so high that it is hard to imagine anyone else clearing it.

Only once has Hamm been part of a team that failed to meet expectations: in 1995 when the U.S. women, the defending champions, finished third at the World Cup in Sweden. It wasn't for lack of effort by Hamm, who was later voted team MVP. In one match, with goal-keeper Briana Scurry ejected and no more subs left, Hamm pulled on the big splayed gloves and marched resolutely into the net. She did not, of course, allow a goal.

So there was, after all, one more mission. To regain the World Cup trophy, at home. The response to the win was immensely different than it was eight years ago, when resounding silence greeted the National Team on its return from winning the inaugural World Championship in China.

Now, the United States is Mia Hamm's personal version of "Cheers." Everybody knows her name. Nike put it on a building at corporate headquarters. Pert used it to sell shampoo. Hamm was voted the most marketable female athlete in the country last year by *The Sports Business Daily*, finishing ahead of figure skaters Michelle Kwan and Tara Lipinski and tennis star Venus Williams. *People* magazine put her among its 50 Most Beautiful.

Mia-mania reigns after nearly every U.S. National Team match, when hundreds of grade-school sopranos sing her name from the sidelines, pleading for autographs. She obliges, over and over. Ambassadorships are supposed to be soft jobs, but Hamm and her teammates are evidence to the contrary.

"We're going to sign for as long as it takes," Hamm said

A very familiar sight: Mia Hamm celebrates after scoring. She recorded her 100th international goal in Rochester, New York, against Russia in 1998. That day she also scored her 101st goal. She has joined Italian players Carolina Morace, with 106 goals, and Elizabetta Vignotta, with 108, as the all-time leading scorers in international games. (Below and opposite photos JBW/International Sports Images)

after a match last June. "Every time we step on the field we know the responsibility we have. We take it very seriously."

She speaks softly. There is a layer of Texas and the Carolinas in her voice and perhaps even a latent hint of Italy, where her father Bill, a retired Air Force colonel, was stationed when she was a little girl.

Being a public figure is somewhat of a discipline for Hamm, a keenly private person. But passion and discipline describe her both on and off the field. To understand what drives her, you first have to understand the experiences that have taught her how precious and temporal life's gifts can be.

Her grandfather and her uncle, a government geologist, were killed in a plane crash on an expedition in Alaska the very week that Hamm made her first appearance for the U.S. team in 1987. She was just 15, the youngest player, male or female, ever to wear a national team uniform.

Hamm went on to glory at the University of North Carolina, where she scored 103 goals and helped win four NCAA titles, taking a year off in midstream to help win the 1991 World Championship.

Shortly before the 1996 Olympic Games, Hamm was rocked again when Navy Admiral Jeremy Boorda, a close family friend for whom Bill Hamm once served as chief advisor, took his own life.

Hamm grieved, then set her focus back on the Olympic Games. She was hobbled by a sprained ankle for much of the tournament but still contributed her share and more, setting up the winning goal in the gold-medal game against China. The 76,489 fans who watched that match in Athens, Georgia, constituted the largest crowd ever to witness a women's sporting event.

After the match, Hamm sought out her family and fell into the arms of her brother, Garrett, her original athletic idol. As it turned out, it would be the last triumph they celebrated together.

Hamm, the third of four girls, distinctly recalls the day she got an older brother. New and strange toys multiplied in the closet: baseballs and gloves, footballs, skateboards. Garrett Hamm was a Vietnam War child, shy and insecure from having lived with three different families by the time the Hamms adopted him at age eight.

Yet he was completely confident with a ball in his hands or at his feet. And when tiny, dainty Mia, named for her mother's favorite dance instructor, followed him to his touch football games, he picked her for his team when no one else would and sent her out on the post pattern.

"She was his secret weapon," said Hamm's mother, Stephanie. "He knew what great hands she had and how fast she was."

Mia followed Garrett into soccer, too, and it will forever be her sorrow that he had to quit while she kept playing.

Garrett Hamm struggled for years with the consequences of a rare blood disorder that forced him to give up the sports he loved. He died at the age of 28 on April 16, 1997, when a fungal infection overtook his weakened immune system two months after he underwent a bone marrow transplant. He left behind a wife and a toddler son.

At the time of the transplant, Mia made the difficult decision to go public to try to raise

Head Coach DiCicco once said of Mia, "Just watching her play is a pleasure. She makes you hold your breath." (Above and opposite photos JBW/International Sports Images)

money for her brother's medical expenses. "I knew that with the financial situation that he was in, it was going to be a struggle," she said. "I was given a gift, and I was willing to do anything to help that. I remember thinking, 'I don't care if I have to beg.' And it was amazing, the response I got." A benefit game between the National Team and a group of college all-stars netted $50,000. The match, now used to promote awareness of the National Bone Marrow Registry, has become an annual tradition called The Garrett Game.

When Garrett died, the National Team was preparing for a belated six-game victory tour to celebrate its Olympic success. Mia requested a leave of absence for the first two matches. She and her family buried Garrett in a quiet ceremony in Wichita Falls, Texas.

Two weeks later, Mia was back, running on the diagonal, ponytail snapping smartly behind her like the colors of a depleted, but still-defiant, brigade. With the pure act of movement, she saluted her brother. In a torrential downpour in Milwaukee, she scored twice and made one assist in the first 16 minutes she was on the field.

She made her point. She always does. She is determined to use the gifts of a healthy body and a healthy spirit to their utmost. In a way, she will always play for two. "When Garrett passed away, there was no bitterness," Hamm said. "He didn't want us to feel guilty. He knew we'd be sad, but he would want us to remember him most by going out and doing the things that he couldn't do and the things we love to do. I'd give up all this in a heartbeat to have him back, just to give him one more day or one more week. But I know Garrett wouldn't want that."

Who else would have kept goal after the U.S. goalie was ejected and all subs had been used? Mia did for 7 minutes vs. Denmark, in the 1995 World Cup. (Phil Stevens Photography) *Opposite:* Mia signs trading cards for her fans. (JBW /International Sports Images)

Throughout Hamm's soccer journey, her teammates have hiked right alongside, never a deferential step behind. They keep her grounded, eliminating the static that can overwhelm an athlete of her stature. They challenge her, they needle her, and several of them are so spectacular in their own right that they keep Hamm from being constantly double-teamed.

After Hamm became just the third player ever to score 100 goals in a U.S. Women's Cup match in Rochester, New York, she made a characteristically modest statement. "The crowd was great, and it was a lot of fun, but it was even better because I could share it with my teammates," she said. "I wouldn't have scored any goals without them, and it's a credit to this team that we can have moments like this."

Her humility is no act. Hamm is one of the least spoiled superstars of the modern age. Yet there's an obvious irony: She has spoiled us forever. Her artistry has become habitual, expected. How many times has she split defenders on the run, or appeared magically in the one spot on the field where no opponent thought to go?

We tend to take her skills for granted.

She doesn't.

We shouldn't. ∎

Bonnie De Simone is a Chicago Tribune *staff writer. Portions of this chapter first appeared in the* Chicago Tribune.

"HAMM IS ONE OF THE LEAST SPOILED SUPERSTARS OF THE MODERN AGE"

GETTING GOALS
DANIELLE FOTOPOULOS AND BECKY BURLEIGH

BY MARK LONG

THE SUN RADIATED THROUGH the North Carolina sky, shining brightly on everything it touched. Patches of bright white clouds barely left their mark on the impeccable blue background. Thousands of fans filed into the University of North Carolina–Greensboro soccer stadium, most wearing T-shirts that screamed "Go Heels!" or proclaimed the dominance of the North Carolina women's soccer program.

University of Florida head soccer coach Becky Burleigh took it all in. She looked up at the sky, gazed at her players, glanced down the sideline at legendary soccer coach Anson Dorrance, and took a deep breath. This excitement, this nervous anticipation, this uncontrollably giddy feeling—so this is what it means to compete for an NCAA Division I-A title.

The 31-year-old soccer coach had guided the fourth-year Florida Gators all the way to the NCAA championship game, where they faced 15-time national champion North Carolina.

Everything seemed to point against a Florida win. The crowd. The history. The talent.

But Burleigh believed in her players. The players believed in Burleigh. And on December 6, 1998, the Florida Gators made history and defeated the North Carolina Tar Heels 1–0 in front of a record crowd of 10,583. Burleigh became the first woman ever to win a soccer national title. The Gators became the first school in 15 years to beat the Tar Heels in an NCAA final and the fourth team ever to win a soccer national title, joining North Carolina, George Mason, and Notre Dame. "When you believe you can win and you put forth the effort, it's gonna happen," Burleigh says. "Where a lot of teams fall short is believing that they can. Our team really believed it could win. We had all the ingredients. We had all the stuff necessary to compete for a national title. It just became a fairy tale."

What unfolded on that crystal clear day in Greensboro, North Carolina, was beyond anything Burleigh could have imagined when she was hired in June 1994 to build the Florida soccer program. She never imagined the promise she made to her first recruiting class—that they

The University of Florida performs the famous gator chomp before winning the 1998 NCAA Final against the University of North Carolina. (JBW/International Sports Images)

Top: The Florida Gators celebrate victory. *Above:* Victorious Danielle Fotopoulos, after scoring in the sixth minute to give the Gators a 1–0 lead; UNC's star Tiffany Roberts is outjumped in the NCAA Final. Tiffany has won two NCAA championships with the Tar Heels and accumulated 67 international appearances. (All photos JBW/International Sports Images)

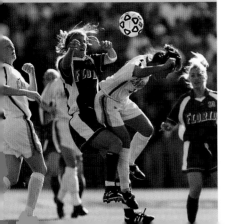

would compete for a national title within four years—would come true. And she never imagined that Danielle Fotopoulos, one of the nation's most promising soccer players, would land in Gainesville as a junior in 1996 to finish out her playing career. All Burleigh really knew when she took the Gators helm was that she would have her players competing for a national title.

In 1994, what did competing for a national title signify? Perhaps making the NCAA Tournament. Maybe being ranked in the Top 25. Or maybe playing host to an NCAA Tournament match. Burleigh would have been happy with any of those results. The Gators finished 14-4-2 in their inaugural season, barely missing a bid to the NCAA Tournament. Burleigh saw her team's potential. And it was greatly magnified when Fotopoulos decided to transfer to Florida.

Danielle Garrett Fotopoulos began her soccer career with Southern Methodist University in 1994. She led the Mustangs in scoring (45 points) and goals scored (20) her freshman season. She led the nation in scoring (83) and goals scored (32) the following season and led the Mustangs to a first-ever Final Four appearance.

She would do the same for the Gators just three years later. Garrett, from Altamonte Springs, Florida, married Tampa-based club coach George Fotopoulos in June 1996. She began her Gators career that summer and made an immediate impact during the 1996 season. "I knew she would score goals," Burleigh said. "And I knew she would be an asset to our program and help us beyond just scoring goals. We knew she'd help us get other people and become more high profile. Plus it was a good challenge for me as a coach to work with someone that has national team experience. I felt we had to provide her the best environment to develop her skills." Fotopoulos led the nation in scoring for a second straight season (81) and racked up Southeastern Conference Player (SEC) of the Year and SEC Tournament Most Valuable Player honors. "I just wanted to get along with everybody and fit in," says Fotopoulos, who scored four goals in nine matches as a member of the U.S. National Team while she attended the University of Florida. "I wanted to play for Florida, but more than anything I just wanted to win."

And the Gators did just that, posting a 22-3 record, claiming the No. 8 seed for the NCAA Tournament and playing host to their first NCAA Tournament matches. But the season came to an end in the quarterfinals, the furthest the program had ever advanced. And it came to an end at the hands of North Carolina in a 9–0 embarrassment in Chapel Hill, North Carolina. That was the first of three meetings in the NCAA Tournament between Florida and North Carolina. Despite the heartbreaking loss, Burleigh netted one of her most talented recruiting classes in 1997, thanks to all the exposure the Gators garnered through their NCAA Tournament run. Andi Sellers, a high school All-American and Florida high school Player of the Year from Satellite Beach, led the class. Sellers set the state goal-scoring mark with 230. Burleigh figured she had a potent starting forward tandem in Sellers and Fotopoulos, who stood just 71 points shy of passing North Carolina's Mia Hamm for No. 1 on the NCAA's all-time career scoring list. But it never happened. Fotopoulos tore the anterior cruciate ligament in her right knee while training with the U.S. National Team in April 1997, four months before the start of Florida soccer practice. She redshirted the 1997 campaign, forced to wait one more season before leaving her mark on NCAA soccer. Without Fotopoulos, the Gators won a second straight SEC crown but only reached the second round of the NCAA Tournament, again falling to North Carolina, this time 5–0.

"Danielle's injury made us better as a team," Burleigh says. "It forced other players to step up." Fotopoulos' return, though, was key for the Gators in 1998. She not only became the all-time scoring leader—male or female—in NCAA soccer history, she guided the Gators to their record-making season. Fotopoulos broke the NCAA goals record with her 104th career goal on October 18, 1998, in a 9–1 win against Mississippi. She racked up honor after honor during her senior season, winning SEC Player of the Week honors twice, SEC Player of the Year honors again, and another spot on the All-American team. And the Gators compiled an 18-1 regular-season record. Their only loss came to North Carolina, a 2–1 overtime setback, in front of a record crowd of 5,222 in Gainesville. But Florida would get another shot at the Tar Heels. This time, after North Carolina ended Florida's hopes at a national title in the NCAA Tournament for two straight seasons, the Gators would be the ones to send the Tar Heels home.

Fotopoulos' presence was key. The Gators survived a 1–0 match against Santa Clara in the NCAA semifinal, and Fotopoulos recorded an assist on Sarah Yohe's match-winning goal. Next up: North Carolina. The Tar Heels had Florida's number. They outscored the Gators 14–0 in two NCAA Tournament matches. They owned a 5-0 all-time record against Florida. The Gators managed to score a combined two goals in those five meetings. But Florida wanted a rematch with the Tar Heels after coming so close in Gainesville. Behind Fotopoulos and goalkeeper Meredith Flaherty, Florida accomplished what some thought was unthinkable. Fotopoulos scored the lone goal in the match at the 5:23 mark on a 20-yard free kick. The kick came off the bottom of the crossbar, just beyond North Carolina goalkeeper Siri Mullinix's outstretched hands, and bounced into the back of the net. It was all Florida needed. Flaherty had eight saves and countless other deflections to thwart each Tar Heels attack. Fotopoulos won tournament offensive MVP honors while Flaherty won tournament defensive MVP honors.

Above: Danielle showcases how matched the Division I record held by Tiffeny Milbrett and Mia Hamm. "Mia is the best player in the world and it's amazing to me that I have reached the same number of goals she had," said Danielle. *Below:* Tiffany Roberts in action in the 1998 NCAA final. *Bottom:* Head Coach Becky Burleigh, the first woman to coach a winning Division I team NCAA championship team. (All photos JBW/International Sports Images)

On the sidelines, Burleigh could barely contain herself. She watched Fotopoulos and Flaherty and the rest of the Gators neutralize No. 1 North Carolina. With two minutes remaining in the match, she began jumping up and down, almost willing the seconds on the clock to tick faster. She jumped and jumped and jumped until the two minutes ran out. Then she looked for anybody to wrap her arms around. She did it. The Florida Gators did it. The Florida players piled on top of one another and cried tears of exhilaration as several North Carolina players fell to the ground, faces buried in their hands, silently weeping. Burleigh's promise to her players came true.

Fotopoulos had ended her collegiate career with a match-winning goal in the NCAA Final. She had ended her career with 284 career points, six points ahead of Hamm, and 118 career goals, 15 ahead of Hamm and Portland's Tiffeny Milbrett. "It seemed like it was our destiny to win the title," Fotopoulos said. "You really can't put your finger on it; it just worked. We really gelled together, and everything went right for us." There in the Carolina sunshine, behind a clear Carolina blue sky and in Tar Heel country, the Florida Gators won their first national championship. "It was just such a perfect ending to a perfect season," Burleigh said. ∎

Mark Long is a graduate student in journalism at the University of Florida.

FINDING A FIELD TO PLAY ON
KELLY SMITH, AWAY FROM HOME
BY MARIE WOZNIAK

KELLY SMITH KNEW IT the first time she kicked a ball. Her father realized once he watched her play. It was only a matter of time before players of all ages would see it too—Kelly had a natural ability for soccer.

Because of this innate talent, Smith has stood apart on the soccer field all her life, from her playing days as a youngster to the present, as a member of England's national team and one of the top college players in the United States, playing for Seton Hall University.

Kelly grew up in Garston Watford Herts, north of London, playing soccer like most other six year olds. When she wasn't kicking the ball against a wall in the backyard or playing soccer with a neighbor in the park, she was watching men's football in the Premier League with her father, Bernard.

When Kelly was seven, there were no girls' teams in her area. Her only choice was to play with the "lads" on her school team and for the Garston Boys Club—where she made an immediate impact.

Kelly completely dominated those games against seven-, eight-, and nine-year-old boys. With her short haircut she blended in with the boys, and no one even thought she might be a girl.

Bernard has remembered, "Many people came to us asking who Kelly was. They would say, 'He's a good little guy.' They were completely astounded when I introduced them to Kelly, they couldn't believe the player they had watched was a girl."

Kelly caused quite a stir with the opposing teams' parents; so much, that some refused to play Garston. "They would say, 'You've got that girl playing again' and wouldn't put their team on the field," said Bernard, who accompanied his daughter to all her games.

"The parents were jealous of me being a girl and being the best player in the park. They didn't want their sons to be beaten by a girl. They wouldn't field their teams to play us, so the only thing for me to do was to leave the team. I was hurt but didn't let it bother me too much. I just did my own thing after that," said Kelly.

Determined to continue playing a sport that came to her so easily, Smith took her skills to the Watford Ladies team. This time the ten year old stood out among women who were more than twice her age and once again faced envious teammates.

"They were a bit taken back that I was so young and could play with them," said Smith,

Twenty-year-old Kelly Smith sidefoots the goalkeeper in an England vs. Scotland match. (Stu Forster, Allsport)

who would go on to play for a number of other women's teams. Among them was the women's team formed by the renowned Arsenal Football Club, whose men's team is in the English Premier League, which was Kelly's favorite team growing up.

Word began to spread about this soccer phenomenon. And at the age of 16, Kelly Smith saw a dream come true. She was asked to train with England's national team. "I knew soccer would play a major role in my life. I enjoy it so much and always dreamt of playing for my country," said Smith, who played her first national team match when she was 17. "I always thought Kelly could play for England and told her so. I was convinced it would happen," said Bernard. "Everything came so natural to her. She's got great vision, balance, and skill."

Smith was attending West Herts College at home when an American coach told her about scholarship opportunities in the U.S. He was a friend of Seton Hall coach Betty Ann Kempf, who promptly contacted Kelly. Kempf then visited the Smiths and impressed upon them the value of an American education and the chance for Kelly to be a part of the growing women's soccer program.

With the support of her parents, Carol and Bernard, Kelly accepted the scholarship offer, making the tough decision to leave home and experience a new culture. "It was very hard. I didn't want to leave my family and friends, but when I heard about the opportunities in America, I jumped at the chance. The main reason was to further my soccer career, as there seem to be many more opportunities for women's soccer in America, especially with the possibility of a professional league."

She battled homesickness early on but overcame that with the help of her new American friends, adjusting to the change and enjoying the new lifestyle. "It was hard to adapt at first. Things are totally different in the United States. I even had problems with the language, because we use other words—nobody understood me. We say *shopping center* and the *cinema* in England, but here it is a *mall* and the *movies*," said Smith in her accent, which makes her stand out even more in New Jersey.

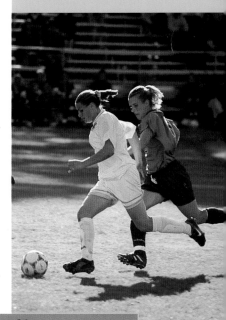

"I've met a lot of good people and made some great friends. I've definitely become more independent living away from home and feel I've grown as a person," said the twenty-year-old Smith. "It's been a wonderful experience."

Smith's life has been greatly affected by the move across the Atlantic, but she's made just as much an impact on the Seton Hall soccer program, bringing excitement to the small campus in New Jersey.

She was the top scorer in the NCAA in her second season, with 24 goals in 17 matches, and ranked second the previous year with 25 goals. Smith has won a number of honors already in her two-year career, including the Big East Conference Offensive Player of the Year Award for both seasons.

With Kelly on the field, Seton Hall reached a new level, winning 25 games over two years, and earning a national ranking for the first time ever.

Smith's skill and speed leave opponents and fans in awe. Her one-on-one skills are tremendous and many of her goals are scored when she makes a 30- to 40-yard run with the ball, beats two or three defenders, weaves between another two defenders and the goalkeeper, and places the ball in the net.

"What she's proved is that she's one of the best players in the world," says Seton Hall coach Betty Ann Kempf. "She never stops amazing us with what she can do. Kelly is an exceptional athlete and has what you'd call a 'soccer mind.' She is the total soccer player."

The differences between England and the United States have also extended to the playing field. "I'm singled out much more over here, and there are always more defenders around me. Although the skill level is better at home, the pace is much quicker in America. Because there is more emphasis on conditioning, the players are more fit and stronger, which makes for a faster game."

Smith has known all along that she possessed a special talent for the game. But being as humble as she is, she never really talked about it, and instead just showed it on the field. "I guess I just have an instinct and know what to do in certain situations. I've watched different players all my life and studied their movements with the ball. Then I would try out those moves to see if they worked."

Kelly Smith has come a long way from those days playing on the boys' teams. And she looks to go even further if her dream of playing professional soccer comes true. But most importantly, Kelly Smith has made the best of a talent she was born with, while playing a game she loves. ■

Marie Wozniak is the Assistant Athletic Director/Communications at Seton Hall University.

MAKING THE GRADE ANN LISSEMAN:

BY PETE DAVIES

*Ann Lisseman is a British policewoman and amateur soccer player in a country unused to
women in either calling. When Pete Davies met Ann in 1995 she was working in Liverpool and
commuting across the north of England to play for the country's preeminent women's team, the
Doncaster Belles. One of England's most respected writers on soccer, Davies followed the team
for a season for his extraordinary book on the women's game,* I Lost My Heart to the Belles
(first published by William Heinemann, 1996; by Mandarin in paperback, 1997).

ANN LISSEMAN WANTED TO PLAY FOOTBALL, catch bad guys, and save the whale, not necessarily in that order. If she could have had one dream fulfilled, it would have been to swim
with a whale—a dream which, when she first heard it, [her teammate] Joanne Broadhurst
mulled over before saying, "I suppose I might go down the beach with a lager and wave at
one." But then PC 5615 Lisseman was a more serious person, and an ambitious one too—taking exam after exam to become a detective, a sergeant, a woman on top in a very male world.

Because in the police the sexist, the racist, the homophobe, they were still all there. She
said sometimes it was horrible, they could be the world's worst; when you got the policeman
that looked down on you as a woman, you didn't half get a hard time. It came in little comments, in condescending behavior, in the way they treated you.

So why did she do it? She did it because she'd always wanted to, since they came with the

POLICE OFFICER, DEFENDER

careers talk when she was 14 at school; she did it because it would change, because it was already changing, because she could see it being addressed and getting better all around her.

She worked in a Crime Support Unit in Birmingham city center, a team responsible for an urban area including the hardest parts of Handsworth, an area with more crime than the whole of Warwickshire. They worked serious and serial crime—armed robbery, murder, anything that needed numbers quickly. They'd picked up four juveniles that week too, four from a gang of six they reckoned were on a string of burglaries; they were 14, 15, the youngest was 11. Eleven years old . . . it was weird, but you got used to dealing with them, it wasn't like all criminals were bad people, there were some you felt sorry for—but . . . just lately two teenagers, they were having an argument and one pulled a knife and the other one pulled a bigger knife, and he chased him down the road and stabbed him in the back and he died, and why? What was the matter with it? Sometimes, she thought, the world was going totally crazy—so when Sunday came she forgot about it, because she had to.

I asked if she ever thought of packing it in and she said, "Yeah. But we all don't want to go to work some days, don't we?"

On a Sunday she took her mind off it with the Belles, and at work they were great about it. They knew she was good, because she'd sometimes played with them on an office team against other police sides, and they'd take her along like a secret weapon. They'd not say anything and she'd see the other lot thinking, "Yah, they've got a girl on their side, what's that?" And she'd go past them and they'd not know what to do then, would they? But she didn't do it any

Ann Lisseman playing for the Belles, in England's Premier League. (courtesy Ann Lisseman)

Above: Sergeant Ann Lisseman of the West Midlands Police Force stationed in Wolverhampton. (courtesy Ann Lisseman) *Below:* Belles' huddle before a match begins; Lisseman battles for the ball. (Sportsphoto) *Opposite:* Belles' subs nervously watch a game's final moments. (Sportsphoto)

more—it got rough and some of them weren't that good, and (more likely out of clumsiness than malice) you could too easily wind up with a broken leg; it wasn't worth it.

Besides, sometimes you did get malice. Some men, they *can't* be beaten, can they? Not by a woman. It terrifies them, the very idea, so then they kick you, and you know damn well they mean it. Or there was one who came to circuit training and in the sprints he ran next to her, and she beat him—and then he was banging his fist on the wall, his head too, going, Oh no, a woman's beat me, a woman's beat me. Dead serious.

She was starting games [for the Belles] now, but it hadn't often been like that; a grafter while others shone, she'd been a perpetual sub. She knew other players were better than her, so fair enough—and sometimes too the pressure of work, of studying to get qualified for promotion, would be so great that she'd not be able to train like she should, and then her fitness would suffer, and she knew it. . . . If there was anything that summed up the Belles it was commitment in their work, commitment in their attitude. Besides, players like Kaz, Gill, Joanne, they weren't just good, they were exceptional, they were such class, and wanted to train anyway to keep up with them, you wanted to work hard—otherwise you just looked stupid.

She kept the commitment in perspective. She ran two or three miles every day that she could, did circuits once or twice a week in the local gym, went two hours each way to training on Wednesday when shifts allowed it—but she wouldn't move to Doncaster to make it easier, she wouldn't muck her career about. She said, "It's not *that* important, is it? I'm sorry, but it isn't. I love football, OK, but I don't live for it. I haven't got a job that allows me to."

On the other hand, if the football wasn't there, "It'd just be like a big hole. It'd be horrible." And because she loved it that much, not starting, being sat on the bench, it wasn't any fun. She knew someone had to do it—but she didn't feel Paul [the Belles' coach] was always quite fair, and one element of her nerves on a Sunday morning was always to do with whether she'd turn up and not get a game, and . . . she didn't know what he was thinking sometimes. . . . She felt she'd worked that hard to get her fitness back up, and . . . he'd said she wasn't fit . . . so now she saw him as a challenge. Not start her, start her and take her off—she'd be damned if she was going to quit on him.

The Belles didn't play for three weeks; their game in Ilkeston was called off because of a waterlogged pitch, the Sunday after that was an England game. But it meant the injuries cleared, and they had Joanne back, so with the exception of Gail Borman, they were near enough themselves again.

They played the Wolves on their training ground, the Miners' Welfare pitch in Stainforth. There was a rough little clubhouse of worn brick and rusted metal, with barbed wire round the roof. Club helpers doled out tea and coffee from big urns. The Belles squeezed into a tight little dressing-room and Paul named the team, and Ann was starting.

It took them 20 minutes to get back into shape against a big Wolves side who had little to offer beyond muscle, lard, and bottle—but of those, they had plenty. Some of the tackling was brutish and Sheila, jogging out to tend one clattered party after another, was angrily surprised to learn that the ref (seeing it was only women's football) hadn't bothered checking studs before the game.

And the Belles stood up to it. On 20 minutes Tina Brannan skipped through a motorway pile-up of challenge by the corner flag, some center-half the size of a redwood lunging helpless through her slipstream as she whipped in the cross, and Coultard was horizontal in the air over the penalty spot, the diving header punched in, the keeper all ends as it flew away off her legs, and after that you knew it was only a matter of time. By halftime Belles were 4–0 up, and by the end it was 6–0, Wolves were falling over all round the park, playing ten in their goalmouth, just a bunch of big bodies, nothing left.

Ann was substituted with 20 minutes to go; Paul sent on a Canadian girl they'd just signed named Bianca Wilkinson from the town of Mission, British Colombia. Ann sat on the bench shrugging.

Afterwards Coultard reminded them about the monthly committee meeting; if there was anything bothering them, anything at all, as player's reps they should go to her. At the bar Ann said quietly, "Well, I started didn't I? Look on the bright side. Starting's a bonus." Then Paul came and had a word with her, told her she'd done all right; he'd taken her off because they were winning and he'd needed a proper look at this Canadian girl, needed to give her enough of the game. So when he'd gone Ann said, "Now I know I didn't do anything wrong. I can go home happy now."

Home happy to study *The Police and Criminal Evidence Act 1984: A Guide for the Practitioner*; she had another exam for sergeant coming up in a month. ■

OPEN YOUR EYES
REFEREEING MEN AND WOMEN
BY JOHN POLIS

SO HERE'S THE SITUATION. Two highly competitive soccer teams are waging a furious battle, each trying to impose its will on the other. Neither team gives an inch. It's win at all cost.

You—the referee—are stuck in the middle. You have one job. Make sure 22 emotionally charged athletes play by the rules. Sounds simple enough. But in reality, a soccer referee has perhaps the most difficult officiating job in sports. In fact, it's hard to believe that there are people who would actually want to referee soccer. Most of us have seen those overseas video clips of the ref being chased around the field by irate players. The fans yell at you. The players, well, they yell at you too. You never get to be the hero. Most of the time, you're the villain. And adding to the macabre nature of this thankless job, you must wear a black outfit.

Now tell me, who wants to do that? Thankfully, for the good of the game, there are some who do. Those who rise through the ranks to officiate at the highest level have more than earned their stripes. They have passed test after test in games involving youth, amateur, high school, college, and professional games.

Today's referees have also started to gain experience officiating both men's and women's games. And while the rules are the same, the goals are the same dimensions and the field is the same size, men and women react differently to situations during the game, according to Sandra Hunt of Bellingham, Washington, one of America's top-level women's referees. An identical situation, says Hunt, may bring different responses depending on whether the players are male or female.

Women referees from around the world are at work. *Top:* Sandra Hunt is an official referee in Major League Soccer. (JBW/International Sports Images) *Center:* Claudia de Vasconcelos in the 1991 FIFA Women's World Cup. (Joyner, Poperfoto) *Above:* Ingrid Jonsson signals a foul, (Martin Venegas, Allsport) *Below:* Nancy Lay refereeing a Major League Soccer match. (JBW/International Sports Images)

Example: An attacking player beats an opposing defender, but is chopped down from the side by a second defender. The referee's whistle blows and out comes the yellow caution card. Comment from the guilty player in the men's game: "Oh, come on, ref! I got all ball on that one! I can't believe you are giving me a card for that!" Comment from the guilty player in the women's game: "Okay, ref, I was late on that one." Even in an international match.

"If a woman fouls someone, she will own up to it," says Hunt, who was a Major League Soccer official in 1998 and was slated for more duty in 1999. "It seems that gamesmanship comes a little less naturally to the guys."

Alfred Kleinaitis agrees that the men are more likely to try and take advantage of a situation." For example, not giving ten yards on a free kick," says Kleinaitis. "With the men, you tell them ten yards and if the referee turns, they'll try and take advantage of it. If you tell the women ten yards, they usually abide by it."

While women may accept referees' decisions somewhat better than men, it doesn't mean they are any less intense or competitive than their male counterparts. "Women are less 'in your face' but they don't disagree any less," says Hunt. "They feel as strongly about a poor decision. But in the heat of competition, they react differently than men."

"When men on the same team are screaming and hollering at each other, it is acceptable to them. With women, that's just not very acceptable. I think it's more cultural than anything else."

Hunt says women players tend to be more sympathetic to their teammates. "A foul against a player is felt by everyone," she says. "You might as well have made the call on everyone."

Men and women react differently to teammates' injuries, Hunt adds. "If a woman is injured, there will be at least one player over there by her immediately. In a men's game, it seems like a player must at least have a limb detached before someone helps him."

Since the FIFA World Championship for Women's Football (the name of the first FIFA women's event) in 1991, women's soccer tactics have become much more sophisticated. Slowly, the dreaded tactical foul has crept into the women's game, something Kleinaitis notices more each year. "Fouls in a women's game are usually honest ones," says Kleinaitis.

"But in watching the NCAA finals this year, there were more fouls than you would have seen eight years ago. Every time there was numerical superiority by one team over another, there was a tactical foul to slow them down."

Besides dealing with the difference in the psychological approach of men and women to soccer, there is a very real difference in the positioning referees take in games, according to Hunt. "The positioning is very different for a women's game. Because I do mostly men's games, you have this pattern of running and you do it without thinking. In a women's game, I have to continually remind myself of my positioning throughout the match."

To position herself for a goal kick in a men's game, Hunt is usually past the halfway line. "In a women's game, I need to be in the same half of the field as the goal kick, opposite my assistant referee. I need to be in the drop zone to have a good view of the next play. "I also make wider runs in a women's game because play is stretched more touchline to touchline. Not always, but often, men's games are played more direct, down the field, due to the strength of the players."

The physical battles within a men's game are well-documented. But what about the physical side of the women's game? "Women like to play a physical game just like the men, but they dislike rough tactics," says Hunt. "The men, they sort of accept that, because they are just more used to that treatment of one another. The women don't mind a late challenge or attempt at the ball, but late hits or bumps from behind are not appreciated."

The bane of all soccer officiating is the referee who, for some reason, thinks that a women's game is easier than a men's game. "A game is a game is a game. A foul is a foul is a foul," says Kleinaitis, who hammers this home in lectures to referees throughout the United States. "If you don't approach every game in a professional manner, you don't have any right to call yourself professional."

Woman referees take the same physical tests as men and must reach the same plateaus regarding numbers of games worked. Major League Soccer (Division I), the A-League (Division II) and the USISL minor league system will continue to be leaders in the effort to have women officiating at the highest level. ■

The rise of women's soccer has created many opportunities for female officials to climb the ladder of success. FIFA announced its intention to use only female officials in the 1999 FIFA Women's World Cup in the United States. "Refereeing is beginning to catch up with the game of soccer in the U.S. Thirty-eight percent of all players in the United States are women. We will continue to work to bring along more quality female officials. There are plans to use more women in Major League Soccer so the future is bright for those who can make the grade." said Al Kleinatis, manager for referee development for U.S. Soccer, who supervises the education and training of more than 100,000 soccer officials throughout all 50 states.

MISSION POSSIBLE . . .
ESPECIALLY WHEN YOU'RE STRONG, TOUGH, AND NORWEGIAN
BY KNUT LANGELAND

Norway's Bente Nordby and Ingeborg Hovland console each other after loosing 2–1 to China in the 1998 Goodwill Games. (Andy Lyons, Allsport)

GRO ESPESETH IS PROBABLY about the closest you get to a female European soccer heroine. In soccer season, she's always hoping—and even believing it is possible—to do what she likes better than anything else in soccer: beat the U.S.

"The rivalry between the United States and Norway goes back a long time, and it is probably more tense and fierce between these two nations than any other. Beating them on their home turf in the World Cup would match anything I've ever experienced," said the then 26-year-old Norwegian veteran in the spring of 1999.

After the Norwegian soccer season ended in October, she spent the rest of the autumn contemplating whether to hang up her boots for good or to continue playing at the highest level for one last season. Her decision to give it 100 percent for one more year spelled bad news for the hosts of the 1999 summer's soccer World Cup. Ever since the U.S. beat Norway 2–1, in the final of the 1991 World Cup in China, Gro Espeseth has been one of the key players on the successful Norwegian soccer team.

Described as the best female defender in the world after Norway won the 1995 World Cup in Sweden, Gro Espeseth has certainly left her impact on the world soccer scene. Her rough and competitive style has earned her a reputation as one of the toughest and most dedicated female players not only in Norway but internationally. In the terminology of the game, she is one of soccer's "hard men." Although there are surely those who would testify differently, Gro Espeseth would never hurt anybody intentionally.

"But sometimes in the midst of all the tension and determination I just get carried away," she has admitted.

Those who meet her only on the soccer field would probably be inclined to judge her as a one-dimensional and single-minded soccer fanatic. But behind that tough appearance is a soft, lovable, and even vulnerable woman, who is almost as uncompromising

Top to bottom: Norway celebrates its 2-0 triumph over Germany in the final of the 1995 FIFA Women's World Cup (Chris Cole, Allsport); Gro's regimen includes time off the field camping (courtesy Gro Espeseth); Bente Nordby, Norway's goalkeeper, lifts the World Cup trophy and exults with her teammates after winning the 1995 final (Chris Cole, Allsport); Norway vs. Denmark: Gro has shouldered Norway's defensive responsibility since 1991 (Andy Lyons, Allsport); Norway crawls to the podium to celebrate their World Cup victory (Bild Byran).

in her will to do good for others as she is in her will to win. In keeping with her good character, she is studying to become a social worker.

"Who I am on the field is not necessarily who I am off the field. Furthermore, a soccer game is played between two teams with individuals who have chosen to do it by their own free will, accepting not only that if one team wins, the other will lose, but also to suffer the pain that this might bring upon them," she points out.

Open and reflective, positive and inspirational, Gro Espeseth has grown to become one of the public favorites on the national soccer scene. She is highly valued not only among teammates and coaches but also among media and sponsors. Originally more shy than outspoken she has made a point of accepting invitations and challenges of all kinds, knowing that every public appearance is an opportunity to grow as a player as well as a person.

Becoming a soccer player was not something she chose for herself. It just happened. She started playing because the other girls in the neighborhood did. They met on a gravel playground just down the road from her house. Gro and her girlfriends blended in with the boys.

By the time Gro was born, women's soccer had been officially introduced into Norway. Interest in this activity gradually grew and it became ordinary to see girls playing the sport together. "For me it was perfectly natural to start playing soccer. It never struck me as strange or unsuitable. All my friends played soccer and I certainly didn't feel like one who contributed to women's liberation or something like that," says Gro. By the time she started playing organized soccer, at the age of eight or nine for the local club Fri, Norway had already played its first few games at national level, the first of which took place in 1978 against Sweden.

Sweden played its first national match in 1973 and was the leading nation in women's soccer for many years. It took nine years and eleven matches before Norway was able to beat the Swedes in 1987 at the European Championships in Oslo.

Despite the growth of the sport over the years and its general acceptance, Gro did face some hindrances. "Even I experienced prejudice in my time. In some areas we still struggle for recognition, but generally we feel welcome in the soccer family. The Norwegian Soccer Federation certainly does its part to give women's soccer the recognition that it deserves." With women's soccer Norway has been able to reach the main stage of international soccer.

Gro never considered herself to be any more talented than the others, and a future with the national team was nowhere near her dreams until it happened.

Before the 1991 season, at the age of 18, she moved from her local club, Bjoernar, to the dominant female soccer club in Bergen at that time, Sandviken. Just prior to that she had made her debut for Norway's junior national team and received widespread recognition for her performances.

In the spring of 1991 she was picked for the first time for the seniors. Starting her top-level, national career as a winger, she was close to sensational, even scoring a couple of goals in her first few matches.

Gro Espeseth has become an international star hardly as a result of God-given talents alone. "I consider myself more a product of hard training, total commitment, and strong willpower. Without the training and the determination, I never would have reached as far as I have," she has said. At the peak of her career she trained almost twice a day, totaling 20 hours a week.

In 92 matches played for Norway since 1991, she has scored seven goals, has become World Champion once, European Champion once, and has won an Olympic bronze medal. But although her career is strewn with victories, honors, and recognition from around the world, she has also experienced profound and utter disappointment. In 1996 she went to Japan to play professionally for the Suzuyo Shimizu Football Club, but the artificial training turf in Shimizu injured her knees and she was forced to give up. Gro was devastated, not so much by her personal failure, but primarily for letting the Japanese down. She returned to Norway after three weeks, without having played a game.

But failing in the European Championships in Norway was the bitterest defeat of all. "I was the captain and felt that I was more responsible than any. Not only did I miss from the penalty spot, I also had a bad performance overall in the decisive quarter final against Italy," she remembers.

Gro Espeseth in tears after the biggest disappointment of her career—that could have been the image she left us with. After the match against Italy in June, she played only one more match for Norway before announcing that she had decided to give up her international career to be able to spend more time with her future husband and his daughter. At 25 Gro Espeseth saw her career drawing to an end, and she was preparing for a life without soccer. She had come to realize that other values counted just as much and even more than the game she loved.

It was a tough decision, and although she was repeatedly approached by the federation, she firmly turned down every request for a comeback until August 1998, when she was persuaded to lend a hand in the final World Cup qualifier against England. Even after that she stood by her decision. But as the season drew to an end she became doubtful. "I've been playing soccer since I was nine, and the thought of giving it up became frightening," she says.

After a week-long holiday and another week of contemplation, she decided to make herself available for the national team again—much to the delight of its coach Per-Mathias Hoegmo. At the same time she decided to leave her old club, Sandviken, to join the most successful club in Norway in the 1990s, Trondheims-Oern. Money has never been a motivation for Gro, and it wasn't this time either, because economically the offer from Sandviken was better. "I left because I wanted to try to win something at club level too," says Gro.

Until three years ago, she hadn't received a dime from the club, and even today only the very best players can expect to be offered salaries at club level. International players have scholarships presented to them by the federation, and Gro today receives an annual contribution of around $13,000, in addition to the rather insignificant fee paid by the club.

"At least it gives me the freedom to study without having to depend on the bank."

Even though women's soccer is still very much in the shadows of men's soccer in Norway, Gro finds no reason to complain. Facing what will probably be her last season at the top level fills her with mixed feelings. "I don't regret anything. I've experienced a lot; learned a lot, both by winning and by losing, and I've gotten to meet a lot of great people all over the world. Soccer has given me opportunities and privileges I could only dream of." ∎

Knut Langeland covers soccer, skiing, and the Olympic Games for Bergens Tidende, *Norway's fourth largest newspaper.*

ANY ROOM FOR A WOMAN?
CAROLINA MORACE: CRUSADER AND COACH

BY SIMONE SANDRI

Above: Milan's Carolina Morace commands the field: with 150 caps and 106 goals with the national team, Carolina has a remarkable record. She stopped playing after the 1997 European Championships in Norway, where her team lost in the final to Germany. *Opposite:* Carolina covers her opponent in an Italy vs. Spain match in 1996. *Following pages:* Milan players in action against Serie A rival Prato. (All photos Richiardi)

ITALY IS HOME TO some of the greatest soccer players in the world. Silvio Piola, the great soccer player of the 1930s and 1940s, and Paolo Rossi and Roberto Baggio, the unforgettable strikers of the 1982 and 1994 World Cups, are just a few of the names in the glorious history of Italian soccer.

More familiar to the recent soccer fan is the backbone of the present Italian national team: such players as Alessandro Del Piero, Christian Vieri, and Paolo Maldini. People in Italy and across the world closely follow their progress both on the field and off, and every couple of years a new star emerges. Yet the enthusiasm for Italian men's soccer generates an obstacle for the women's sport. Few foreign soccer aficionados, and even fewer Italian ones, have delved into the current Italian soccer scene to look for a female figure with comparable technique, grace, and tenacity.

Carolina Morace, who has showcased her incredible talent on the soccer field for more than two decades, and who has became a reference point for women in all sports, is a name that only rings a bell for those few who have seen her commentate on men's Serie A matches on TV or have occasionally read about her in the papers. "I am appreciated and respected more outside of Italy than I am inside," she has told *La Gazzetta dello Sport*. Hardly any attention has been paid to the woman who has won twelve championships with seven different teams. To find another figure with such dominance in world soccer is almost impossible.

Until she decided to call it quits, in June 1998, one could always predict the winning team would be Carolina's. On the field, she was creative and aggressive; off the field, she was equally competitive and inspiring. She started playing for a simple reason, the one that should drive all athletes to the field—the love of the game. Carolina didn't have role models; she just liked the sport. But playing soccer in the 1970s for a woman wasn't the easiest thing. There were not many teams around and, especially, not many people willing to teach the sport to the so-called "weaker sex."

Yet there was absolutely nothing weak with the way the women were playing. The only problem was their training methods. In those days not many coaches were prepared to coach women at that level, and, consequently, practice routines were too often inappropriate. The league wasn't bad, a lot of good foreign players would come to play in the 14 teams of the Italian Serie A, but the women's soccer scene in Italy was moving slowly.

Carolina never complained and took it upon herself to make things better, pushing herself and her teammates and showing great leadership at a very young age. "I don't even recall how I got started," says Morace, remembering the 1970s. "All I know is that since I can remember I always liked soccer. I started playing competitively when I was 11 years old and I reached the national team at 14." That's right, 14 years old. Nowadays that might not seem incredible, considering how young gymnasts, swimmers, and tennis players on the international scene can be.

But in 1978 it was something out of the ordinary, and even more impressive was the fact she was playing for a team in which most of her teammates were over 27. A situation that might have seemed traumatic was routine for a teenager already showing signs of greatness. "I was good enough to stick around with those women," she smiles , "so I didn't feel a stranger at all."

Carolina's career on the soccer field, however, was anything but normal: 153 caps with the national team, 105 goals, 12 Scudetti (Italian Championships), 4 Italian Cups, and 13 scoring titles. On the national team, the Azzurre, she played alongside Betty Vignotto, the other legendary player in Italian women's soccer, and together they made history. "Playing with Betty was something extraordinary," adds Morace, "we complemented each other so well. We always knew where the other one was on the soccer field and we both were really unselfish. It was all about the team and not who would score or who would get her name in the paper."

Carolina now has more trophies than her Roman home can hold. Just recently the International Football Federation of Football History and Statistics voted her the Best European Player of this century, second to Heidi Mohr. And she is not done yet. In 1998 she took on another challenge by becoming the head coach of one of her former teams, Lazio. Together with her team she is chasing yet another goal: winning her thirteenth championship as head coach. Her players look for leadership in her and have learned never to be satisfied, always to want more. Carolina also has the distinction of being the first female graduate of the Academy of Coverciano, the "Harvard of soccer," where professional coaches get their degrees.

Coverciano is a sort of mythological name for Italian soccer fans. In this quaint little town in the heart of Tuscany, soccer is taught and learned by the best. Without a *patente*, the license given by the academy, it is not possible to coach at the professional level or even at the best amateur level. There are many requirements for acceptance to the school. Not too many years ago, the idea of a woman being admitted to Coverciano was unthinkable, but now thanks to Carolina Morace the sex barrier even in the Mecca of Italian soccer has been broken. "I am proud of what I have accomplished," says Carolina, "but we have to change the mentality of the Italian sporting system in which women are still given too little space. In my case I was offered to coach a men's team (in Italy's Interregionale, which is the first division of amateur soccer), but strangely I wasn't even contacted for the women's national team job. I then decided to coach Lazio and things are going great." Her leadership and knowledge are making the transition from player to coach easier for her.

Carolina works side by side with the Minister of Equal Opportunity in order to promote and better the female sporting scene in the country. Moreover, she reached another milestone by becoming the first woman to be an analyst on a soccer show broadcasted by TMC, one of the major networks in Italy. "I had no problem in this field either. I am happy to be looked up to as the one who broke the ice, but there is still a long way to go." Player, coach, reporter, or politician, Carolina Morace is a success story for Italy—and for women. ▪

Simone Sandri collaborates with the New York office of La Gazzetta dello Sport.

SAMBA SOCCER
PURE SOCCER, PRETINHA'S WAY

BY LUCIA NOVAES

SHE IS A WOMAN, she is black, and she plays soccer in Brazil, where apparently the sport was invented for men to play. Delma Gonçalves, nicknamed Pretinha, has managed to overcome prejudice and is now the symbol of Brazilian women's soccer.

Pretinha is 24 and the youngest of seven children (four boys and three girls) raised by Osvanir Gonçalves, a construction worker, and Ana Rosa, a housewife. She grew up in Senador Camará, a poor neighborhood in Rio de Janeiro, and only completed studies through the sixth grade.

At seven she began playing on a clay field with all the boys in her neighborhood. Many believe she developed her great skills and courage by playing with them. She learned to do what she does best—confront her opponents without retreating.

At 14 she went to play on a team called Medanha, from Campo Grande. As a shy 16-year-old, she began playing for Nova Iguaçu and was called to play for the national team. The turning point in her career came a little bit later when the head coach of the Vasco da Gama team, Helena Pacheco, saw her play in Nova Iguaçu. Pacheco recruited her to play for Vasco da Gama, and with them, Pretinha won three Brazilian championships.

"Pretinha is a phenomenon," says Pacheco. "She is gifted and can work well with both legs. I don't know any other player, male or female, who has such skill in this respect. But Pretinha is not only talented, she has the physique and the stature to play aggressively and gracefully at the same time. She is fit as hell and has enough energy to play in every position. Tactically speaking she is exceptional," boasts her coach.

Regardless of whether Pretinha is at the beach or indoors, soccer seems to always be on her mind. She practices every morning and sleeps in the afternoon. She plays indoor soccer competitively in São Paulo at Sabesp and has even won the indoor soccer league three times. Beach volleyball is her hobby. Every once in a while she plays a game with her friends.

This natural ability to play and her love for the game have improved her lifestyle. With more money she has been able to give support to her family and relatives, including 11 nephews and nieces. She has moved into an apartment with two other teammates and friends and has a brand new car and a cellular phone.

Along with the money came offers from other teams, including Japan. But Pretinha's close friendship with Coach Pacheco kept her from taking off the Vasco da Gama jersey. And even though she is happy with what she has accomplished in Brazil, she does have some complaints: "Women's soccer has gone a long way since the 1996 Atlanta Olympic Games but there is still a long road ahead." Professionally and technically the Brazilian team has grown, but they still need to improve and expand its program to increase the team's potential.

Since finishing in fourth place at the 1996 Olympic Games, the Brazilian women have been granted some privileges that might allow them to improve along the way. Now they can also use Granja Comary, the same training facility the men's team uses to train for the World Cup and international championships. The camp is in Teresópolis, a mountain village near Rio, and has the most modern equipment and venues. There is also a special training program for the 2000 Olympic Games in Sydney, prepared by the CBF.

The team must prove itself in order to make people believe in its future. Brazil finished ninth in

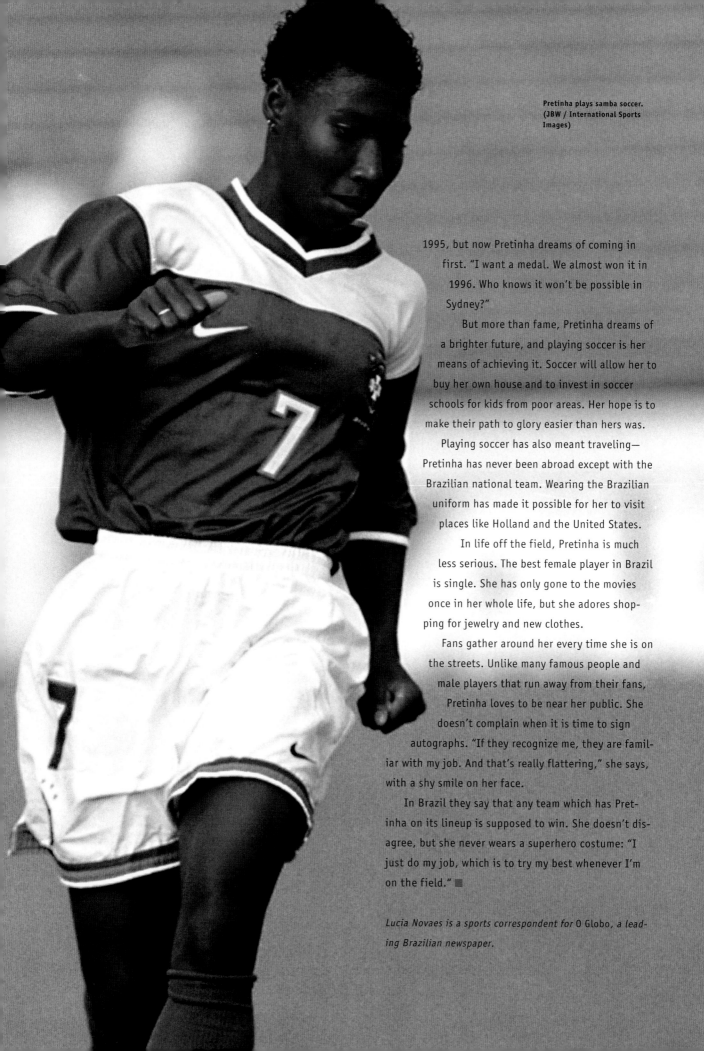

Pretinha plays samba soccer.
(JBW / International Sports
Images)

1995, but now Pretinha dreams of coming in
first. "I want a medal. We almost won it in
1996. Who knows it won't be possible in
Sydney?"

But more than fame, Pretinha dreams of
a brighter future, and playing soccer is her
means of achieving it. Soccer will allow her to
buy her own house and to invest in soccer
schools for kids from poor areas. Her hope is to
make their path to glory easier than hers was.

Playing soccer has also meant traveling—
Pretinha has never been abroad except with the
Brazilian national team. Wearing the Brazilian
uniform has made it possible for her to visit
places like Holland and the United States.

In life off the field, Pretinha is much
less serious. The best female player in Brazil
is single. She has only gone to the movies
once in her whole life, but she adores shopping for jewelry and new clothes.

Fans gather around her every time she is on
the streets. Unlike many famous people and
male players that run away from their fans,
Pretinha loves to be near her public. She
doesn't complain when it is time to sign
autographs. "If they recognize me, they are familiar with my job. And that's really flattering," she says,
with a shy smile on her face.

In Brazil they say that any team which has Pretinha on its lineup is supposed to win. She doesn't disagree, but she never wears a superhero costume: "I
just do my job, which is to try my best whenever I'm
on the field." ■

Lucia Novaes is a sports correspondent for O Globo, *a leading Brazilian newspaper.*

The U.S. Women's National
Team trains the goalkeeper.
(M. Powell, Allsport)

FAMILIAR ANONYMOUS ECSTASY
A STORY ABOUT PERFECT PLEASURE
BY JULIA NAPIER

From Perfect Pitch, *edited by Simon Kuper and Marcela Mora y Aranjo. First published in paperback in 1998 by Headline Book Publishing, London.*

TIPPANIA (TIP OR TIPPI to everyone—hounded as "Tippi Longstocking" on the playground and for that reason never seen with hair past her ears) . . . loved sports: kickball, baseball, touch football. But soccer was her game. Her parents had signed her up to play in the city's first girls' league when she turned five because it seemed like a good alternative to day-care. And Tip had loved it right away. She coveted her uniform: a maroon T-shirt with a soccer-ball patch sewn on the sleeve and her number (28) ironed crookedly on the back, plastic Mitre cleats, and an elusive pair of shinguards with plastic sticks you could take out (and lose, of course). Mostly, however, Tip loved to play—the race to chase the ball down when it was nearly impossible to keep in bounds, . . . the smack it made on the inside of her foot when she actually managed to pass, and rare suspended moments in front of the goal when she shot with all her childish muscles into the net—or the goalie or the bushes. . . .

It was clear early on that Tip was good, good enough to play center-midfield and almost never come out. She felt a vague pride in not hearing her name called as the whistle blew for subs, but mostly she just wanted to stay in, to run more, to fall and get up. It was always thrilling and terrifying and different. She could only describe soccer as a good feeling. It felt good the way mint chocolate-chip ice cream tasted good. . . . Her unmediated devotion to playing soccer, and not to some abstract notion of the game, drew people to her in ways neither they nor Tip understood. Her life emanated from this one perfect pleasure, and so she became perfect to others—if only in those flying green seconds of pass and trap and goal.

Tip continued to play soccer. She grew into an accomplished (if not brilliant) student, a pretty (though not beautiful) young woman, and an exquisite soccer player. This is not to say that she was the most skilled or the most successful player anyone had ever seen. She got cut from the state team after two weeks of practice because the coach couldn't watch her play. On most days, she merely distracted him; but, on others, when she was really on, he wept all down his clipboard—and he cut her from the team. She was good enough to school two thirds of the other girls (or boys or whomever) on the field, but she lacked the silent, feral instinct of a true striker. She inevitably screwed up set plays because they bored her, and she had trouble staying in position. But no matter where Tip was, she was wonderful. On attack, she relaxed before the nervous full backs and slipped almost apologetically past them: slipped, swiveled, doubling all of her joints as her hips rolled in an improbable undulant loll. Coaches often reproached their defenses for having turned to "Swiss cheese" before her diaphanous fakes, but it was more as if they just melted as she dribbled through.

There was just nothing like her. People regularly commented on the sidelines that she looked as if she were "playing under water" and moving through some gelatinous bubble alongside her teammates. . . . No one could take their eyes off her, though the refs learned early on to ignore her altogether if they wanted to call the game remotely well. . . . Scoring didn't interest her that much, but the defense usually lost its mark under her Bermuda Triangle charisma, and someone was always there to receive her steady passes. She did enjoy, however, the occasional full volley or header on an open goal: the twin thunk and swish of a body to ball to net.

Such was the stuff her greatest goal was made of, scored her senior year in high school. . . . This particular day was a Friday, and, as schoolwork didn't beckon, a few of the girls decided to stick around for a game of seven-on-seven with the boys team in the wide late-summer

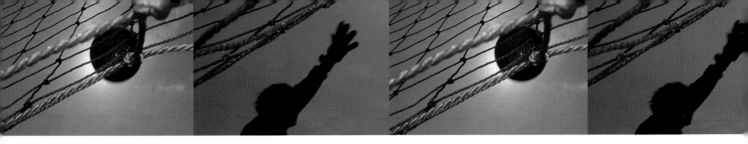

night. While both varsity teams did well in their respective leagues, the girls were truly excellent and the boys solidly average. This inequality levelled the field of play between the sexes, and the games were usually close—plus lots of tight flirtatious marking.

After about twenty minutes, things were zigzagging along: skins 3, shirts 2. Everyone was breathing hard with sprints and giggles in-between goals and come-hither slide-tackles. Right after the skins scored for the third time, the shirts won a corner. Tip could feel the goal coming as Molly waited to take the kick. She hovered calmly at the back post and hopped a few languid steps forward as the ball lofted towards the edge of the six-yard box. Greg, her marker, was already hypnotized by the supple swerve of her feet that he left her alone and, instead, marked the post she had abandoned. As the other girls jockeyed and pushed, she took one more step to the right and soundlessly left the ground. Just before the ball flew directly into her abdomen, she swung to the left in a gorgeous swoop and sent the black and white object of her affection directly into the lower right corner of the goal.

It slayed the entire skins team, and the game ended immediately: a "next-goal-wins agreement" that had never been agreed upon. The boys just evaporated in embarrassed desire. The shirts, used to playing in a mixed crowd with Tip, rolled their eyes into the boys' direction and began to gather up their things. A little dizzy from her victory, Tip chose to spend the last gusts of the daylight taking a few shots on goal. While her friends chirped off towards the parking lot, Greg fiddled with his Adidas bag, wanting very much to leave; but he couldn't help watching her: three even steps, the right foot curling, unfurling, smack, and a lazy jog to the open goal.

"I'll play goal—if you want?" Greg asked indifferently.
"Sure."

Tip was not unpleased. She had had a crush on Greg for a year, but this term they hadn't had any classes together, and she thought she lost her chance. . . . He rarely watched the girls' team play, but, when he did, it was to watch Tip. Her body, in easy conversation with the ball, enthralled

him. He wanted to play with her, to play next to her, to be near the girl she became on the field.

Tip worked him out as best as possible, shooting high and hard into the corners. Entirely in her element, she teased him by turning conventional penalty shots into coy one-on-one contests. It drove him mad to see her dribbling that sibilant dance towards the goal, and, after about five minutes, he came straight off his line, didn't see her shoot past him, and kissed her at the edge of the penalty box. . . .

Though they broke up a few months later (at the end of the season), Tip didn't realize that all her relationships with men would be forever entangled with her sport. Even when she met someone off the field, he soon became devoted to her on-field persona. It began to complicate things. . . .

College was a particularly difficult time. Tip got scouted by many of the top Division I schools, but all of the coaches left her game perturbed or in tears. She was too distracting for the big time and ended up starting at a lesser Ivy League power. Tip felt relief at this demotion; winning the national championship meant nothing to her and playing on TV even less. The game would be easier and more personal on a less conspicuous team. . . .

Homecoming weekend of her sophomore year, an entire fraternity stopped at the field in the midst of a pubcrawl. They were already drunk and tired by noon, and the women's game seemed like a good excuse to collapse in the grass. The second half had just begun, Tip's favorite moment in the game: finally really ready to play with forty-five minutes left to enjoy. . . . Hovering near the halfway line, she trapped a goal kick with her chest (her favorite trap) but managed to pop the ball up as she slowed its force, headed it twice over two defenders, brought it sweetly to the ground, passed it off, received it again, hung the stopper out to dry, and was about to score when the sweeper took her out with one loud swipe from behind. Penalty. Tip always took their penalties for an obvious reason. It was all in the set-up: a slow walk to set the ball down, swivel, jog back, one long look into the

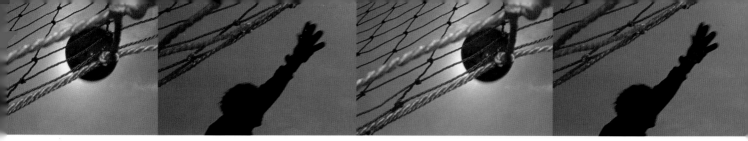

doomed goalie's eyes and an instep pass into the corner. It never failed, and the whole fraternity went to pieces. One of them made it to his feet and cheered: "Number 13 we love you!" Some rolled and sobbed in the grass, and others passed out from the double intoxication of beer and Tip.

Nothing was ever the same after that day. Men swarmed their games and serenaded Tip from the sidelines. . . . Of course, some of the attention was flattering, but Tip had never wanted to be an actress, and she felt now as if she were performing at every match: a captive performer to a coercive audience and all of her super soccer sisters soon began to hate her.

It had been sort of funny at first, and the other women imagined that they, too, had inspired the increased attendance at their games. They soon lost their delusions and privately, in groups after practice, gossiped bitterly about Tip's "egotistical exhibitionism." Tip dreaded going to practice, and started to dress in her dorm room in order to avoid the middle school cold shoulder of her teammates. She asked her friends not to come to her games and began to fake injuries in order to stay on the bench as long as possible. . . .

Tip had been trying to remove herself piecemeal from the team. Never before in her whole life had anything separated her from the pure play of the game. . . . More than anything, she felt lonely, lonely for the familiar and anonymous ecstasy of playing. . . .

The following Saturday, in an aggressively close game against Amherst, with a record 600 spectators in attendance, Tip ended it. In the thirty-seventh minute of the first half, fans roaring "Tippania! Tippania!" Tip stopped the ball cold at the halfway line, bent sharply down, picked it up in her hands and walked off the field through the silenced crowd. The ref didn't blow his whistle, the coaches didn't protest, and her teammates did not call after her. . . .

Tip stopped playing that day, that minute. She didn't know what to do but disappear, to step off the balcony and leave her frenzied suitors empty-mouthed. The change in routine itself was devastating. She stayed late in the library or went for runs, trying to fill the hours in some productive way, but she still heard the gallop of cleats and the high calls of "mark your girl!" Her friends called and invited and chatted, but Tip was amazed with loneliness. . . .

Tip graduated from college, moved to Brooklyn with some girls from school, and worked for a few years at an architectural firm. Living with friends in one of the greatest cities in the world suited her just fine.

Tip ran several times a week in the park in Brooklyn. As soon as it got warm, small pick-up games would compete for space in the frayed fields where she ran in the evening. She always stopped to watch and rest a little. . . . She envied them everything. . . . Entirely unnoticed by the roller-blading jogging passers-by, the men shed the stilted posture of life beyond the pitch and eased into motion. They played.

Tip stood at the edge of the field, dying to join them. Unable to stop herself, she walked towards them.

"Excuse me, could I play with you all?"

"You play?"

"Yeah, I play a little."

Laughter from the two teams.

"Sure, play over here."

They noticed nothing at first because no one passed to her. But Tip had waited too long for this moment and, craving the light touch of the leather against her skin, won the ball and scored.

Wonder, lips parting, imagine that, God—she's beautiful. . . . For five or ten minutes, they played together. . . . The guys played their own game, inviting her slight swift body into the fast-passing dance. And then, it slowly fell apart. All they wanted was to watch her play. Tip felt the change on the field. It was like the transition from being drunk and happy to being drunk and sick. She was sick and frustrated and furious. . . . She walked quickly to the key chain she had dropped at the edge of the pitch, strode straight to the ball, opened the pocket knife and punched the blade into the cheap leather. ■

Julia Napier grew up in Atlanta and is a former top-level soccer player.

LIFE WITHOUT FOOTBALL would be a death, too. I see myself at 60, hair pure white, still too long, my hips on the waiting list, my face and arms deeply creased. My kneecaps pop out every quarter of an hour but I have learned how to squeeze them back into place without fuss. . . . Then someone sneers and says, "What's that bloody granny doing on the pitch?" And I smile as I slide in, steal the ball off him and potter down the pitch to score yet again.

—Alyson Rudd, *Astroturf Blonde*

1999 FIFA WOMEN'S WORLD CUP

MATCH #	SCORE	STADIUM	MATCH #	SCORE	STADIUM
1 USA v DEN	3:0	GIANTS STADIUM	22 CAN v RUS	1:4	GIANTS STADIUM
4 BRA v MEX	7:1	GIANTS STADIUM	23 CHN v AUS	3:1	GIANTS STADIUM
6 CHN v SWE	2:1	SPARTAN STADIUM	24 GHA v SWE	0:2	SOLDIER FIELD
7 JAP v CAN	1:1	SPARTAN STADIUM	21 NOR v JAP	4:0	SOLDIER FIELD
5 AUS v GHA	1:1	FOXBORO STADIUM	18 GER v BRA	3:3	JACK KENT COOKE
8 NOR v RUS	2:1	FOXBORO STADIUM	19 NGA v DEN	2:0	JACK KENT COOKE
3 GER v ITA	1:1	ROSE BOWL	20 MEX v ITA	0:2	FOXBORO STADIUM
2 DPK v NGA	1:2	ROSE BOWL	17 USA v DPK	3:0	FOXBORO STADIUM
12 NOR v CAN	7:1	JACK KENT COOKE	28QF CHN v RUS	2:0	SPARTAN STADIUM
16 AUS v SWE	1:3	JACK KENT COOKE	27QF NOR v SWE	3:1	SPARTAN STADIUM
15 JAP v RUS	0:5	CIVIC STADIUM	25QF USA v GER	3:2	JACK KENT COOKE
14 CHN v GHA	7:0	CIVIC STADIUM	26QF BRA v NGA	4:3	JACK KENT COOKE
12 BRA v ITA	2:0	SOLDIER FIELD	29QF USA v BRA	2:0	STANFORD STADIUM
9 USA v NGA	7:1	SOLDIER FIELD	30SF NOR v CHN	0:5	FOXBORO STADIUM
11 DPK v DEN	3:1	CIVIC STADIUM	31SF BRA v NOR	0:0 (5:4 PK)	ROSE BOWL
10 GER v MEX	6:0	CIVIC STADIUM	32F USA v CHN	0:0 (5:4 PK)	ROSE BOWL

OFFICIAL FIFA THREE-LETTER DESIGNATIONS: AUS–Australia, BRA–Brazil, CAN–Canada, CHN–China, DEN–Denmark, GER–Germany, GHA–Ghana, ITA–Italy, JAP–Japan, DPK–Korea, MEX–Mexico, NIG–Nigeria, NOR–Norway, RUS–Russia, SWE–Sweden, USA–United States

GROUP A	GROUP B	GROUP C	GROUP D
USA	GERMANY	NORWAY	CHINA PR
KOREA DPR	BRAZIL	JAPAN	AUSTRALIA
NIGERIA	MEXICO	CANADA	GHANA
DENMARK	ITALY	RUSSIA	SWEDEN